COST MANAGEMENT: TEXT AND CASES

COST MANAGEMENT: TEXT AND CASES

Data Ram Joshi

CYBER TECH PUBLICATIONS
4264/3, Ansari Road, Daryaganj, New Delhi-110002 (India)
Ph.: 011-23244078. Fax: 011-23280028
E-Mail: cyberpublicationsdelhi@yahoo.com

COST MANAGEMENT: TEXT AND CASES

Data Ram Joshi

First Edition 2009

Published by :

G.S. Rawat for **Cyber Tech Publications**
4264/3, Ansari Road, Daryaganj, New Delhi-110002 (India)
Ph.: 011-23244078. Fax: 011-23280028
E-Mail: cyberpublicationsdelhi@yahoo.com

Printed at : A

Preface

The primary principle of cost management is that costs do not simply happen; they are the results of management decisions. To prevent mistakes and identify opportunities, cost management focuses on anticipating the impacts of alternative decisions. HMS combines value-chain, activity-based costing, value-added analyses, activity-based management, and economic value added to build a logical and easily communicated view of cost management. This proactive cost management perspective motivates all the topics of the book. This approach is not as radical as it might seem. More and more companies are adopting cost management in one way or another, and complementary business curricula (e.g., marketing, management, and operations) have embraced the approach.

Each chapter develops its concepts and applications in the context of a focus company, which is closely based on the actual practices and experiences of a real company. Although the focus organizations are disguised and not real themselves, they are realistic and motivate students by making their study cost management more tangible and interesting. Focus companies reduce abstract, conceptual discussions and communicate the decision-making context of cost management. It allows grounded, logical descriptions of the origins of cost management problems and their solutions. The text has a balance of manufacturing, service, government, mature, and start-up focus companies to demonstrate that the concerns of cost management are universally applicable.

The focus-company context also shows that strategic, cross-cultural, international, technological, or communication issues really do complicate concepts that at first seem straightforward. However, cost management contributes reliable principles that guide managers toward successful solutions. Many companies, of all sizes and industries, have embraced team-based decision making. This is having a profound effect on the role of individuals who previously may have had predominantly functional roles and loyalties. Effective cost managers participate in team decision making and understand how to work with individuals from different cultures and functional backgrounds. The text prominently features team decision making with emphases on interaction and communication.

—*Author*

CONTENTS

1

Introduction

Cost Management is the process whereby companies use cost accounting to report or control the various costs of doing business.

The term cost management is widely used in business today. Unfortunately cost management has no uniform definition. Cost management generally describes the approaches and activities of managers in short run and long run planning and control decisions that increase value for customers and lower costs of products and services.

For example, managers make decisions regarding the amount and kind of material being used, changes of plant processes, and changes in product designs. Information from accounting systems helps managers make such decisions, but the information and the accounting systems themselves are not cost management.

Cost management has a broad focus. It includes – but is not confined to – the continuous control of costs. The planning and control of costs is usually inextricably linked with revenue and profit planning. For instance, to enhance revenues and profits, managers often deliberately incur additional costs for advertising and product modifications.

Cost management is not practiced in isolation. It is an integral part of general management strategies and their implementation. Examples include programs that enhance customer satisfaction and quality as well as programs that promote new product development.

Many cost management concepts are inevitably intertwined with manufacturing and production concepts, such as lean accounting, value chain analysis, throughput accounting, theory of constraints, etc.

COST OVERRUN

Cost overrun is defined as excess of actual cost over budget. Cost overrun is also sometimes called "cost escalation," "cost increase," or "budget overrun." However, cost escalation and increases do not necessarily result in cost overruns if cost escalation is included in the budget.

Cost overrun is common in infrastructure, building, and technology projects. One of the most comprehensive studies [1] of cost overrun that exists found that 9 out of 10 projects had overrun, overruns of 50 to 100 percent were common, overrun was found in each of 20 nations and five continents covered by the study, and overrun had been constant for the 70 years for which data were available.

For IT projects, an industry study by the Standish Group (2004) found that average cost overrun was 43 percent, 71 percent of projects were over budget, over time, and under scope, and total waste was estimated at US$55 billion per year in the US alone.

Spectacular examples of cost overrun are the Sydney Opera House with 1,400 percent, and the Concorde supersonic aeroplane with 1,100 percent.

The cost overrun of Boston's Big Dig was 275 percent, or US$11 billion. The cost overrun for the Channel tunnel between the UK and France was 80 percent for construction costs and 140 percent for financing costs.

Three types of explanation of cost overrun exist: technical, psychological, and political-economic. Technical explanations account for cost overrun in terms of imperfect forecasting techniques, inadequate data, etc. Psychological explanations account for overrun in terms of optimism bias with forecasters. Finally, political-economic explanations see overrun as the result of strategic misrepresentation of scope and/or budgets.

All of the explanations above can be considered a form of risk. A project's budgeted costs should always include cost contingency funds to cover risks (other than scope changes imposed on the project). As has been shown in cost engineering research, poor risk analysis and contingency estimating practices account for many project cost overruns.

Numerous studies have found that the greatest cause of cost growth was poorly defined scope at the time that the budget was established. The cost growth (overrun of budget before cost contingency is added) can be predicted by rating the extent of scope definition, even on complex projects with new technology.

Cost overrun is typically calculated in one of two ways. Either as a percentage, namely actual cost minus budgeted cost, in percent of budgeted cost. Or as a ratio, viz. actual cost divided by budgeted cost. For example, if the budget for building a new bridge was $100 million and the actual cost was $150 million then the cost overrun may be expressed as 50 percent or by the ratio 1.5.

OPTIMISM BIAS

Optimism bias is the demonstrated systematic tendency for people to be over-optimistic about the outcome of planned actions. This includes over-estimating the likelihood of positive events and under-estimating the likelihood of negative events.

Experimental Demonstration

Armor and Taylor review a number of studies that have found optimism bias in different kinds of judgement. These include:

- Second-year MBA students overestimated the number of jobs they would receive and their starting salary.
- Students overestimated the scores they would achieve on exams.
- Almost all the newlyweds in a US study expected their marriage to last a lifetime, even while aware of the divorce statistics.
- Professional financial analysts consistently overestimated corporate earnings.
- Most smokers believe they are less at risk of developing smoking-related diseases than others who smoke.

Students in one study rated themselves as much less likely than their peers (students of the same sex at the same college) to experience negative life events such as developing a drink problem, having a heart attack, being fired from a job or divorcing a few years after getting married.

Optimism bias does not apply universally. For example, people overestimate their chances of experiencing very low-frequency events, including negative events.

Effects of Overconfidence

Example : Increased Risk Taking and Insufficient Preventive Care

Optimistic overconfidence bias can induce people to underinvest in primary and preventative care and other risk reducing behaviors, like abstinence from smoking.

Example : Credit Card Borrowing and Penalty Rates and Fees

Overconfidence causes many individuals to grossly underestimate their odds of making a payment late. Statistically, many people are quite likely to make at least one or more payments late due to the normal range of difficulties and delays in day-to-day life. Overconfidence bias causes these individuals to grossly underestimate the odds of this happening, and therefore to accept grossly punitive fees and rates (for example an interest rate of nearly 30 %) as a result of otherwise minor transgressions like a late payment.

Other companies now have extended on this approach, by increasing interest rates to punitive rates for any late payment even if it is to another creditor. Overconfidence bias makes these terms more acceptable to borrowers than if they were accurately calibrated.

Overconfidence bias also causes many individuals to substantially underestimate the probability of having serious financial or liquidity problems -for example from a sudden job loss or severe illness. This can cause individuals to take on excessive debt under the expectation that they will do "better than average" in the future and be readily able to pay it off.

Overconfidence, Locus of Control and Depression

Overconfidence bias may cause many individuals to overestimate their degree of control as well as their odds of success.

This may be protective against depression -since Seligman and Maier's model of depression includes a sense of learned helplessness and loss of predictability and control. Depressives tend to be more accurate, and less overconfident in their assessments of the probabilities of good and bad events occurring to them. This has caused some researchers to consider that overconfidence bias may be adaptive and/or protective in some situations.

Optimism Bias and Planning

Optimism bias arises in relation to estimates of costs and benefits and duration of tasks. It must be accounted for explicitly in appraisals, if these are to be realistic. Optimism bias typically results in cost overruns, benefit shortfalls, and delays, when plans are implemented.

The UK government explicitly acknowledges that optimism bias is a problem in planning and budgeting and has developed measures for how to deal with optimism bias in government (HM Treasury 2003). The UK Department for Transport requires project planners to use so-called "optimism bias uplifts" for large transport projects in order to arrive at accurate budgets for planned ventures (Flyvbjerg and Cowi 2004).

In a debate in Harvard Business Review, between Daniel Kahneman, Dan Lovallo, and Bent Flyvbjerg, Flyvbjerg (2003) – while acknowledging the existence of optimism bias – pointed out that what appears to be optimism bias may on closer examination be strategic misrepresentation.

Planners may deliberately underestimate costs and overestimate benefits in order to get their projects approved, especially when projects are large and when organizational and political pressures are high. Kahneman and Lovallo (2003) maintained that optimism bias is the main problem.

Mechanisms

A brain-imaging study found that, when imagining negative future events, signals in the amygdala, an emotion centre of the brain, are weaker than when remembering past negative events. This weakened consideration of possible negative outcomes is one possible mechanism for optimism bias.

REFERENCE CLASS FORECASTING

Reference class forecasting predicts the outcome of a planned action based on actual outcomes in a reference class of similar actions to that being forecast. The theories behind reference class forecasting were developed by Daniel Kahneman and Amos Tversky. They helped Kahneman win the 2002 Nobel Prize in Economics.

Kahneman and Tversky (1979a, b) found that human judgment is generally optimistic due to overconfidence and insufficient consideration of distributional information about outcomes.

Therefore, people tend to underestimate the costs, completion times, and risks of planned actions, whereas they tend to overestimate the benefits of those same actions. Such error is caused by actors taking an "inside view," where focus is on the constituents of the specific planned action instead of on the actual outcomes of similar ventures that have already been completed.

Kahneman and Tversky concluded that disregard of distributional information, that is, risk, is perhaps the major source of error in forecasting. On that basis they recommended that forecasters "should therefore make every effort to frame the forecasting problem so as to facilitate utilizing all the distributional information that is available" (Kahneman and Tversky 1979b, p. 316).

Using distributional information from previous ventures similar to the one being forecasted is called taking an "outside view." Reference class forecasting is a method for taking an outside view on planned actions.

Reference class forecasting for a specific project involves the following three steps:

- 1. Identify a reference class of past, similar projects.
- 2. Establish a probability distribution for the selected reference class for the parameter that is being forecasted.
- 3. Compare the specific project with the reference class distribution, in order to establish the most likely outcome for the specific project.

Whereas Kahneman and Tversky developed the theories of reference class forecasting, Flyvbjerg and Cowi (2004) developed the method for its practical use in policy and planning. The first instance of reference class forecasting in practice is described in Flyvbjerg (2006). This was a forecast carried out in 2004 by the UK government of the projected capital costs for an extension of the Edinburgh Tram.

The promoter's forecast estimated a cost of £255 million. Taking all available distributional information into account, based on a reference class of comparable rail projects, the reference class forecast estimated a cost of £320 million. Since the Edinburgh forecast, reference class forecasting has been applied to numerous other projects in the UK, including the £15 (US$29) billion Crossrail project in London. After 2004, The Netherlands, Denmark, and Switzerland have also implemented various types of reference class forecasting.

In 2005, the American Planning Association (APA) endorsed reference class forecasting and recommended that planners should never rely solely on conventional forecasting techniques:

"APA encourages planners to use reference class forecasting in addition to traditional methods as a way to improve accuracy. The reference class forecasting method is beneficial for non-routine projects... Planners should never rely solely on civil engineering technology as a way to generate project forecasts" (the American Planning Association 2005).

Before this, in 2001 (updated in 2006), AACE International (the Association for the Advancement of Cost Engineering) included Estimate Validation as a distinct step in the recommended practice of Cost Estimating (Estimate Validation is equivalent to Reference class forecasting in that it calls for separate empirical-based evaluations to benchmark the base estimate):

"The estimate should be benchmarked or validated against or compared to historical experience and/or past estimates of the enterprise and of competitive enterprises to check its appropriateness, competitiveness, and to identify improvement opportunities...Validation examines the estimate from a different perspective and using different metrics than are used in estimate preparation." (AACE International 2006)

In the process industries (e.g., oil and gas, chemicals, mining, energy, etc. which tend to dominate AACE's membership), benchmarking (i.e., "outside view") of project cost estimates against the historical costs of completed projects of similar types, including probablistic information, has a long history (Merrow 1990). These company's must make a profit from their asset investments and therefore cannot afford the biases in public and government sponsored infrastructure projects.

A NEW TECHNIQUE OF COST ALLOCATION

Cost-Allocation Method

A common cost is a cost of operating a facility, activity, or like cost object that is shared by two or more users. The common cost is lower than the individual cost to each user. The goal is to allocate common costs to each user in an equitable way on the basis of the individual costs of the cost object. Consider Jason Stevens, a graduating senior in Seattle who has been invited to a job interview with an employer in Albany.

The round-trip Seattle-Albany airfare costs Rs.1,200. A week later, Stevens is also invited to an interview with an employer in Chicago. The Seattle-Chicago round-trip airfare costs Rs.800. Stevens decides to combine the two recruiting trips into a Seattle-Albany-Chicago-Seattle trip that will cost Rs.1,500 in airfare. The Rs.1,500 is a common cost that benefits both prospective employers. Two methods of allocating this common cost between the two prospective employers are the stand-alone method and the incremental method.

Stand-Alone Cost-Allocation Method

The stand-alone cost-allocation method uses information pertaining to each user of a cost object as a separate entity to determine the cost-allocation weights. For the common cost airfare of Rs.1,500, information about the separate (stand-alone) round-trip airfares (Rs.1,200 and Rs.800) is used to determine the allocation weights:

Incremental Cost-Allocation Method

The incremental cost-allocation method ranks the individual users of a cost object in the order of users most responsible for common cost and then uses this ranking to allocate cost among those users.

The first-ranked user of the cost object is the *primary user(also called the primary party)* and is allocated costs up to the costs of the primary user stand-alone user. The second-ranked user is the *first incremental user (first incremental party)* and is allocated the additional cost that arises from two users instead of only the primary user. The third-ranked user is the *second incremental user (second incremental party)* and is allocated the additional cost that arises from three users, instead of two users, and so on.

To see how this method works, consider again Jason Stevens and his Rs.1,500 airfare cost. Assume the Albany employer is viewed as the primary party. Stevens' rationale is that he had already committed to go to Albany before accepting the invitation to interview in Chicago. The cost allocations would be:

Cumulative Costs	**Party Allocated**	**Costs Allocated**
Albany (primary)	Rs.1,200	Rs.1,200
Chicago (incremental)	300 (Rs.1,500 -Rs.1,200)	Rs.1,500
Total		Rs.1,500

Albany employer is allocated the full Seattle-Alb any airfare. The unallocated part of the total airfare is then allocated to the Chicago employer. If the Chicago employer had been chosen as the primary party, the cost allocations would have been Chicago Rs.800 (the stand-alone round-trip Seattle-Chicago airfare) and Albany Rs.700 (Rs.1,500 -Rs.800). When there are more than two parties, this method requires them to be ranked a first to last (say, based on the date on which each employer invited the candidate interview).

Under the incremental method, the primary party typically receives the highest allocation of the common costs. No surprise that most users in common-cost situations prefer be an incremental party! In some cases, the incremental users are newly formed companies or a company's new subunits, such as a new product line or a new sales territory Chances for their short-run survival may be enhanced if they bear a low allocation of the common costs.

When both parties are viewed as primary parties, there is no incremental party. If there is a large common cost that must be incurred, using the incremental method can cause the parties to dispute who is the incremental party. One approach in such situations is to use the stand-alone cost-allocation method.

Another approach is to use the *Shapley value* which considers each party as first the primary party and then the incremental party. From the calculations shown earlier, the Albany employer is allocated Rs.1,200 as the primary party and Rs.700 as the incremental party, for an average of Rs.950 (Rs.1,200 + Rs.700)

The Chicago employer is allocated Rs.800 as the primary party and Rs.300 as the incremental party, for an average of Rs.550 [(Rs.800 + 300)2]. The Shapley value method would allocate. to each employer, the average of the costs allocated as the primary party and as incremental party—that is, Rs.950 to the Albany employer and Rs.550 to the Chicago employer.

As our discussion suggests, allocating common costs is not clear-cut. That is why managers should always exercise judgment when allocating common costs rather than blindly follow one method or another. Disputes over how to allocate common costs are often encountered. The next section discusses the role of cost data in various types of contracts. This is also an area in which disputes about cost allocation frequently arise.

COST ALLOCATIONS AND CONTRACTS

Many commercial contracts include clauses based on cost accounting information. For example:

A contract between the Department of Defense and a company designing and assembling a new fighter plane specifies that the price paid for the plane is to be based on the contractor's direct and overhead costs plus a fixed fee.

A contract between an energy-consulting firm and a hospital specifies that the con-sulting firm is to receive a fixed fee plus a share of the energy-cost savings arising from implementing the consulting firm's recommendations.

Contract disputes arise often, usually with respect to cost allocation. The areas of dispute between the contracting parties can be reduced by making the "rules of the game" explicit and in writing at the time the contract is signed. Such rules of the game include the defi-nition of allowable cost items; the definitions of terms used, such as what constitutes direct labor; the permissible cost-allocation bases; and how differences between budgeted and actual costs are to be accounted for.

Supply Chain Management: Transforming Supply Chains into Integrated "Value Systems"

Two years after taking on a challenging job as director of business processes in advance purchasing, Rick Calabra, a General Motors executive, stretched back in his chair thinking about what had transpired between him and the group vice president of Worldwide Procurement (WWP). Rick had been nominated to lead the cluster called "Sourcing and Supplier Management" in General Motor's (GM's) major "Order to Delivery (OTD)" initiative.

This new initiative would radically re-define the business processes at GM. In a presentation, the VP had challenged him to develop a supply base that "can transform end customers' clicks" on GM's Buyer Power Website into technology and demand requirements that are "sensed" by suppliers throughout GM's supply chain via Supply Power (an Internet-based technology for sharing information with key suppliers). A cross-functional team consisting of 50 people representing seven clusters had been put together to take the automotive giant's OTD initiative forward.

GM defines its OTD initiative as:

"The engine that will deliver the promise of e-business to our customers and shareholders by:

- Helping to transform GM from a traditional make-and-sell company (push system) to a dynamic sense-and-respond company (pull system)
- Integrating and streamlining the entire supply chain (supply, manufacturing, and distribution)
- Enabling GM to meet dealer and customer requirements rapidly and reliably."

One of the challenges of the OTD initiative was to develop the capability to quickly deliver customized vehicles to customers ordering them from the GM Buyer Power website.

This task was daunting, as GM's order to delivery lead times for customized orders have historically been 12 to 16 weeks. Rick had been assigned responsibility for the supply part of the initiative. Although this was an exciting project, Rick also realized he had a tough job ahead of him. The problem was complex. How would he get 12,000 suppliers to collaborate on this effort?

Rick realized that the first step involved establishing a dialogue with suppliers. This would help him discover what problems they faced with the OTD initiative. Then, he could recommend solutions to improve supply chain reliability and responsiveness and align it with OTD's vision of "sense and respond."

It was 6 p.m. on a cold winter evening. As Rick looked out of his window, it was snowing. The office building was silent, as most employees had left early due to a snow storm warning. Rick rested his face on his palms and thought to himself, "Where do I start? Will I get cooperation from the suppliers? Can I complete my task within three years?" He was known in GM as a go-getter; the new assignment was a challenge and he had to find the answers.

In the last two decades, managers have witnessed a period of change unparalleled in the history of the world in terms of advances in technology, globalization of markets, and stabilization of political economies. With the increasing number of world-class domestic and foreign competitors, organizations have had to improve their internal and external processes rapidly in order to stay competitive.

DEFINING SUPPLY CHAINS

Faced with the challenge of the current e-commerce-powered competitive environment, organizations now find that it is no longer enough to manage their own business but also the supply chain.

They must be involved in managing the network of all upstream firms that provide input (directly or indirectly), as well as the network of downstream firms responsible for delivery and after-market service of the product to the customer. For purposes of this book, we define the terms supply chain and supply chain management as follows:

The supply chain encompasses all organizations and activities associated with the flow and transformation of goods from the raw materials stage, through to the end user, as well as the associated information flows. Material and information flows both up and down the supply chain.

KAIZEN COSTING

Kaizen Costing is widely used by Japanese organisation as a mechanism for reducing and managing costs.

Kaizen is the Japanese terms for making improvements to a process through small incremental amounts, rather than through large investments.

The major difference between target and Kaizen costing is that target costing is applied during the design stage whereas Kaizen costing is applied during the manufacturing stage of the product life cycle. With target costing the focus is one the product, and cost reductions are achieved primarily through product design. In contrast, Kaizen costing focuses on the production process and cost reduction are derived primarily through the increased efficiency of the production process.

Therefore the potential cost reductions are smaller with Kaizen costing because the products are already in the manufacturing stage of their life cycles and a significant proportion of the costs will have become locked-in.

The aim of Kaizen costing is to reduce the cost of components and products by a pre-specified amount. Monden and Hamada (1991) describe the application of Kaizen costing in a Japanese automobile plant. Each plant is assigned a target cost reduction ratio and this is applied to the previous year's actual costs to determine the target cost reduction. Kaizen costing relies heavily on employee empowerment.

They are assumed to have superior knowledge about how to improve processes because they are closest to the manufacturing processes and customers and are likely to have greater insights into how costs can be reduced. Thus, a major feature of Kaizen costing is that workers are given the responsibility to improve processes and reduce costs. Unlike target costing it is not accompanied by a set of techniques or procedures that are automatically applied to achieve the cost reductions.

INTRODUCTION TO JAPANESE MANAGEMENT PRACTICES

In this discussion David Russell and Ashok Patel examine the major concepts behind Japanese Management and its emphasis on a cost reduction culture rather than cost control. The discussion is centred around the Toyota Kanban production system as an example of Japanese management and discusses the interrelated concepts of:

Kaizen:	Continuous improvement
JIT:	Just-In-Time
Jidoka:	Automation
Shojinka:	Flexible workforce
Soikufu:	Creative thinking

Japanese management is the practice of cost aware management or lean management to a greater or lesser degree as originally adopted by Japanese companies and now being adopted (at least in part, e.g., Just-In-Time) by many Western companies.

Kharbanda and Stallworthy (1991) are of the opinion that one of the factors contributing to the Japanese miracle has been their management practices, but these do not appear to have received much attention in the literature. The situation has recently improved and more literature is now becoming available, especially on Just-In-time (JIT), De Bono (1991) observes:

> *"The Japanese search for quality in manufacturing is unending because, no matter how good something is, there is always the possibility of doing it better. But the Western habit of critical thinking means that first we must find faults and then seek to put them right, so anything without faults is impossible to improve."*

As an example of Japanese management, we will consider the framework of the Toyota Kanban PULL system of production which was adopted by many Japanese companies after the 1973 oil crisis. Throughout the discussion on the Toyota production system, our main reference has been Monden's (1989) article "Framework of the Just-In-time production system".

The rationale of the system is to produce the type of units needed in the quantity needed at the time they are needed. The fulfilment of this objective eliminates all the unnecessary intermediate and finished product inventories.
Kanban (PULL) system of production

In a conventional production system units are pushed through the factory, beginning with plans for material requirements and ending with finished goods. Each production compo nent has a desigated routing, where the preceding part of the production process supplies the subsequent part. Hence the term "PUSH" manufacturing system.

No consideration is given as to whether the next production process is ready to accept the production component. This may result in stockpiles of production components at certain bottlenecks within the factory.

In a "PULL" system of production, nothing is produced until units are withdrawn from final assembly. A component or finished part would remain at a workstation in the production line until the next production process is ready to "PULL" it in. As a consequence, final assembly will determine the nature and timing of all operations. This will ultimately feed back to purchasing and supply.

The result of this is that components or finished parts would not be stockpiled around bottlenecks in production. Moreover, if a preceding production process does not have a component or finished part ready to be pulled into the next production process, workers in this subsequent process will have to wait, highlighting problems in manufacturing which must be resolved.

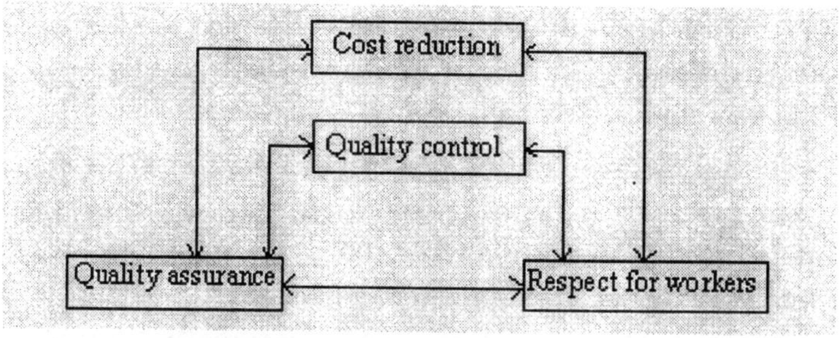

Figure: Primary and secondary goals of Toyota production system

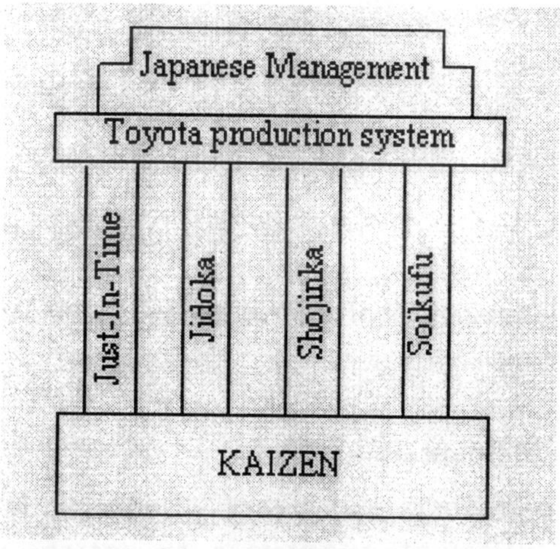

Figure: Composite framework of Toyota production system

TOYOTA PRODUCTION SYSTEM

The primary goal of the Toyota production system is cost reduction, which is conditional upon and interconnected with the secondary goals of quantity control, quality assurance and respect for workers.

The purpose of the secondary goals is that quantity control enables adaptation to daily and monthly demand fluctuations in terms of quantity and variety. Quality assurance ensures transfer of only defect-free units from preceding to subsequent processes. Respect for workers is a prerequisite for the full use of the available human resource necessary for achieving the cost objectives.

The four essential concepts of the Toyota production system are Just-In-Time (JIT), Jidoka, Shojinka, and Soikufu and are built on the foundation of Kaizen. Each is a complete framework in itself (Figure 2). Just-In-Time

Just-In-Time (JIT) is a waste reduction and improved management control framework. The CIMA official terminology defines JIT as:

> *"A technique for the organisation of work flows, to allow rapid, high quality, flexible production whilst minimising manufacturing waste and stock levels".*

CIMA identify two distinct aspects of JIT:

(i) JIT purchasing; matching of material purchasing with usage resulting in near zero levels of stock holding.

The Japanese approach to JIT recognises important procurement issues:

(a) *purchasing;* delivery of materials occurs in sufficient quantities to satisfy immediate requirements only;

(b) *quality at source;* there is no safety net of spare inventory.

(ii) JIT production; a system linked to the Kanban PULL system of production described earlier, whereby each component in a production process is only produced when it is required by the subsequent production process.

The aim of JIT is to deliver the required production items, at the required quality in the required quantities, at the time they are needed. JIT seeks to achieve the following:

(a) zero inventory;

(b) zero defects;

(c) zero breakdowns;

(d) elimination of non-value added activities (e.g., set ups and lead times);

(e) delivery of production items on time 100% of the time.

Shigeo Shingo (1987) points out that the real waste lurks in the forms that do not look like waste. Robinson (1991) mentions seven categories of waste as identified by Toyota. Out of these, the waste arising from overproduction is different because it provides a blanket cover for and hides other wastes. Inventory conceals wastes arising from unreliable suppliers, poor quality of raw material or production, absenteeism, machine breakdowns, long setup times or lead times and idle time and idle capacity from unbalanced processes.

The tactical approach of JIT is to reduce inventory until a problem appears, deal with it and then start further reduction in inventory, thereby exposing previously invisible waste. It never stops trying to make further improvements and thus is a valuable part of the Kaizen framework. Jidoka

Jidoka (autonomation) is a framework of quality assurance. It recognises the disruption and costs caused by defective units flowing on to subsequent processes and thus provides for an autonomous status to defect control. This means that every worker is vigilant about quality and has an autonomous power to stop the whole assembly line if necessary to prevent a defective unit flowing into good production. It supports JIT by never allowing a defective unit to go on to a subsequent process.

Jidoka coupled with a PULL system of production ensures that problems arising in any part of the system will result in production being immediately halted as earlier parts of the production line would not receive the pull instruction from the later stages. Contrast this with a traditional system of production where buffer stocks would allow production to continue, possibly resulting in production problems remaining hidden or unsolved.

Shojinka (flexible workforce) is a framework for efficient utilisation of human resources. It aims at preventing idle time and boredom by employing the twin strategies of:

(i) multiprocess holding; and

(ii) multiskilled worker.

The worker is trained to be multiskilled and the layout of machines is arranged so that a worker might (say) be able to operate three types of machines, for example a lathe, milling machine and drilling machine at the same time.

As workers become multiskilled, they are better able to understand and participate in the total system of a factory and experience greater job satisfaction. Being multiskilled also improves teamwork as it increases the opportunity to assist each other. Soikufu

Soikufu (creative thinking) is a framework for harnessing the creative abilities of employees and a recognition of the fact that no one appreciates a task better than the person who performs it day in day out. Through implementations such as Quality Circles and Suggestion Schemes, employees are encouraged to continuously think about improvement. Soikufu, thus, is an integral part of the overall Kaizen framework. Kaizen

Kaizen (continuous improvement) is the underlying framework of continuous im provement. There are three requirements for a successful implementation of Kaizen. Work organisation and operating practices must expose new improvement opportunities, every employee should be inspired to want overall improvement and employees should be trained in practical problem solving techniques enabling them to make the improvement.

The key points here are that improvement is an on going rather than a one off activity and the employees are motivated to want and possess the essential skill to participate in the improvement activities. Masaaki Imai (1986) observes that the Kaizen concept is crucial to understanding the difference between the Japanese and Western approaches to management.

The most important difference between Japanese and Western management concepts is Japanese Kaizen and process-oriented thinking against the West's innovation and result-oriented thinking.

Cost reduction is thus built into the Japanese approach to management while accounting procedures are used to reinforce management strategies, linking accounting practices and corporate goals and not merely for measuring what is happening (Kharbanda and Stallworthy, 1991).

Many Japanese companies continue to use direct labour hours as the basis for full costing, justified by management as creating the desired strong pro-automation incentive throughout the organisation (Morgan and Weerakoon, 1989).

The significance of cost is not lost however. Japanese management focuses on design and pre-production stages where the majority of a product's total costs are committed. A *target* cost is determined based on the expected price to be paid by the market to achieve a certain market share and sales volume.

The required profit margin is then deducted from the anticipated selling price to arrive at the target product cost. A product of acceptable quality is then designed within that cost. Target costing has a long history in Japan (Kato 1993) of over 30 years. According to Sakurai (1989) more than 80% of the major companies in assembly type industries in Japan have already adopted it.

This emphasis on cost is further enhanced by the management philosophy that *cost is everybody's business* (Kharbanda and Stallworthy, 1991).

THE IMPLICATIONS FOR MANAGEMENT ACCOUNTING SYSTEMS

Management accounting systems inevitably require modification to reflect the evolution from traditional manufacturing approaches to Japanese management philosophies.

Contemporary management accounting systems must place greater reliance on the capture and reporting of information to identify and monitor such criteria as supplier reliability, percentage of deliveries on time, defect rates and set up times. Much of this data is non-financial and is unlikely to be reconciled in the same way as financial data. This may result in difficulties for data capture and problems concerning the reliability and verifiability of the same.

CONCLUSION

The major strength of the Japanese approach is the recognition of human creativity. As Taiichi Ohno, who pioneered the Toyota Production System said:

> *"Manpower is something that is beyond measurement. Capabilities can be extended indefinitely when everybody begins to think".*

Cost aware and creative employees, just-in-time production, autonomous quality assurance and an in-built flexibility in the process layout and employee skills, are dominant features of the Japanese management approach which creates a cost aware and quality conscious culture across the organisation. It has a flexible outlook, encourages improvement and invests in training multi-skilled employees. Japanese management practitioners are arguably better equipped and well suited to face the open-ended challenges of rapidly changing technology and increasing global competition.

CASH-BASED ACCOUNTING RATIOS -BREAKING THE SILENCE

The merits of cash based financial reporting ýÿ for example, it is based principally on facts rather than problematic accounting measurements ýÿ have been known for many years.

However, it was not until 1990 (revised 1996) that the Accounting Standards Board made the publication of Cash Flow Statements (FRS 1) a standard requirement for UK companies. FRS 1 tells us that the ýÿcash flow statement in conjunction with a profit and loss account and balance sheet provides information on financial position and performance as well as liquidity, solvency and financial adaptabilityýÿ. Wise words, but what do they mean?

The usefulness of financial statements is enhanced by an examination of the relationship between them; also by comparisons with previous time periods, other entities and expected performance.

Value can be further added through the calculation and interpretation of accounting ratios. An examination of accounting textbooks and the pages of accounting periodicals reveals an enthusiasm for rehearsing the potential of ýÿaccounting ratiosýÿ demonstrated through calculations of the net profit margin, return on capital employed, current ratio and a host of other "traditional" measures based on the contents of the profit and loss and balance sheet. But what about the cash flow statement? We have seen that its publication was required by the ASB in order to improve the informative value of published financial information. Indeed, some say it is the most important financial statement. One based on "hard facts" which has helped prevent financial machinations such as those that are believed to have occurred at companies such as Polly Peck in the 1980s.

The lack of attention to cash flow-based ratios in accounting textbooks is particularly surprising given their acknowledged role in credit rating assessments and in the prediction of corporate failure. In these and other contexts, the traditional ratios suffer from the same defect as the financial statements (the profit and loss account and balance sheet) on which they are based.

Such ratios are the result of comparing figures which have been computed using accounting conventions and guestimations. Given the difficulty of deciding the length of the period over which a fixed asset should be written off, whether the tests which justify the capitalisation of development expenditure have been satisfied, the amount of the provision to be made for claims under a manufacturer's twelve month guarantee (to give just a few examples), ratios based on such figures are also bound to have limited economic significance. This is not to suggest that the traditional ratios are irrelevant. Clearly this is not so, as they reveal important relationships and trends that are not apparent from the examination of individual figures appearing in the accounts. However, given the fact that cash flow ratios contain at least one element that is factual (the numerator, the denominator or both), their lack of prominence in the existing literature is puzzling.

SOME RECOGNITION OF CASH FLOW RATIOS

The importance of cash flow ratios was dramatically demonstrated, early on, by W. H. Beaver whose 1966 study showed that the most effective predictor of corporate failure was the ratio of cash flow to total debt. Indeed, one of his most surprising findings was that the current ratio proved to be one of the least useful ratios in predicting impending collapse. The importance of cash as an indicator of continuing financial health should not be surprising in view of its crucial role within the business. Colourfully described as a compan's life-blood, a strong cash flow will enable a business to recover from temporary financial problems whereas future negative cash flow will cause even an apparently sound enterprise to move towards liquidation. Expressing the importance of cash differently: a company which descends into a loss-making position often succeeds in making a comeback; one which runs out of cash is unlikely to have a second chance.

Another US-based writer, Yuji Ijiri, has noted the paradox between the way in which investment decisions are made by business and other entities and the way in which the results of those decisions are evaluated. The principal focus for informed investment decisions is cash flows, whether the capital project appraisal method is payback or one of the more sophisticated discounted cash flow-based techniques, namely net present value and internal rate of return. Turning to performance evaluation, however, the emphasis usually shifts to techniques such as return on investment. The inconsistency between the two approaches is highlighted by the use of depreciation cost allocation for computing ROI; a calculation which has no place whatsoever in the above project appraisal methods. Ijiri persuasively argues, therefore, the importance of making project appraisal and performance evaluation consistent.

In the remainder of this paper are presented:

- ratios which link the cash flow statement with the two other principal financial statements;

- ratios and percentages based entirely on the contents of the cash flow statement.

For each ratio is presented both the calculation and a discussion of its significance. Inevitably, there will be some overlap in the messages conveyed by the various ratios presented. This may be due to similarities in the nature of the calculations or to the fact that the results of just one company are used for illustration purposes. The application of the same ratios to different financial facts might well yield additional valuable insights.

Ratios which link the cash flow statement with the two other principal financial statements

Cash flow from operations to current liabilities

$$\text{Cash flow from operations to current liabilities} = \frac{\text{Net cash flow from operating activities} \times 100}{\text{Average current liabilities}}$$

Where:

Net cash flow from operating activities is taken directly from the cash flow statement published to comply with FRS 1. Average current liabilities are computed from the opening and closing balance sheet.

This ratio examines the liquidity of the company by providing a measure of the extent to which current liabilities are covered by cash flowing into the business from normal operating activities.

The ratio is thought to possess some advantage over balance sheet-based ratios such as the liquidity ratio as a measure of short-term solvency. This is because balance sheet ratios are based on a static positional statement (the "instantaneous financial photograph") and are therefore subject to manipulation by, for example, running down stock immediately prior to the year end and not replacing it until the next accounting period. Balance sheet based ratios may alternatively be affected by unusual events which cause particular items to be abnormally large or small. In either case, the resulting ratios will not reflect normal conditions.

Cash recovery rate

$$\text{Cash recovery rate (CRR)} = \frac{\text{Cash flow from operations x 100}}{\text{Average gross assets}}$$

Where:

Cash flow from operations is made up of "net cash flow from operating activities" together with any proceeds from the disposal of long-term assets. Gross assets is the average gross value of the entit's assets.

Assets are required to generate a return which is ultimately, if not immediately, in the form of cash. The CRR is, therefore, a measure of the rate at which the company recovers its investment in fixed assets. The quicker the recovery period, the lower the risk. You may have noticed that the CRR is thus the reciprocal of the pay back period used for capital project appraisal purposes assuming projects have equal (or roughly equal) annual cash flows.

Cash flow per share

Cash flow per share =

Cash flow

Weighted average no. of shares

There are two versions of cash flow reflecting different applications of the cash flow per share calculation:

Version I: Where cash flow = operating profit plus non-cash adjustments such as depreciation and amortisation of fixed assets.

This version provides a measure of the amount of cash that a company generates from operating activities, exclusive of working capital changes. It draws attention to the important role of non-cash adjustments in this process. A company may be operating at a low profit or even a loss and still be capable of generating a significant amount of "cash flow".

Version II: Where cash flow = net cash flow from operating activities + "returns on investments and servicing of finance" taxation and dividends paid. This version recognises the fact that cash is available for long-term investment only after working capital requirements, tax and dividends have been met. It indicates the ability of the company to fund long-term investment out of resources generated internally.

In either case, the number of shares used as the denominator should be the weighted average of the number in issue during the year. However, the average only needs to be weighted if there is an issue of shares involving an inflow of resources; in the case of a bonus issue (where no extra resources are generated), the number of shares post bonus issue should be used without weighting and the number in issue the previous year made comparable.

Capital expenditure per share

$$\text{Capital expenditure per share} = \frac{\text{Capital expenditure} \times 100}{\text{Weighted average no. of shares}}$$

Where: Capital expenditure = net investment (purchases less sales proceeds) in fixed assets.

This ratio, in conjunction with cash flow per share (Version II) can be used in order to obtain a broad indication of whether a business is a net generator of cash or whether it is "cash hungr".

Debt service coverage ratio

$$\text{Debt service coverage ratio (DSCR)} = \frac{\text{EBITDA}}{\text{annual debt repayments and interest}}$$

Where: EBITDA = Earnings before interest, tax, depreciation and amortisation.

The purpose of this ratio is to help assess the ability of a company to meet debt repayments and interest out of cash flow generated from operations. A feature of this ratio is that it is forward looking with the denominator representing expected future cash flows. (If available, the numerator should also be prospective.)

It is seen to be superior to traditional methods used by banks to analyse risk of exposure to debt finance such as interest cover.

A drawback of interest cover is that, as conventionally applied, it is backward looking. Also, it takes no account of capital repayments which, of course, can vary considerably depending on the period of the loan repayment.

Cash flow adequacy ratio

$$\text{Cash flow adequacy ratio (CFAR)} = \frac{\text{Annual net free cash flow (NFCF)}}{\text{annual debt repayments}}$$

Where NFCF = EBITDA minus capital expenditure, interest, tax and preference dividends.

This is a measure widely used in the United States which, in common with the DSCR, attempts to redress some of the weaknesses of traditional analytical ratios through taking a dynamic view of a compan's credit quality by capturing the extent and direction of future financial changes.

The calculation of the ratio is based on estimates for the forthcoming five years. Working capital changes and equity dividends are not adjusted in computing NFCF on the grounds that management has considerable discretion, in the short term, concerning working capital levels and dividend policy. The outflows included in NFCF are, therefore, those judged to be unavoidable. The company has no option but to pay interest, tax and preference dividends; also, it must incur capital expenditure in order to maintain its competitive position.

The significance of the ratio is as follows: the higher the CFAR, the more financial pressure the company is able to withstand before its financial stability and therefore its credit rating is eroded.

Published accounts of Tamari plc for year ended 31 December 1999

Cash Flow Statement	1999	1998
	£000	*£000*
Operating profit	501	420
Depreciation charges	660	600
(-)Increase/decrease in stocks	305	250
(-)Increase/decrease in debtors	184	220
Increase in trade creditors	420	120
Net cashflows from operating activities	1,092	1,610
Returns on investment and		
servicing of finance Interest paid	150	50

Taxation paid	130	110
Capital expenditure and financial investment		
Purchase of tangible fixed asset	1,620	900
Equity dividends paid	160	160
Cash outflow before financing	968	390
Financing		
Issue of loan	1,000	100
Increase in cash	32	290

Profit and Loss Account extracts	1999	1998
	£000	*£000*
Operating profit for 1999	501	420
Interest paid	150	50
Profit before tax	351	370
Taxation:	125	115
Profit after tax	226	255
Dividends paid and proposed	175	175
Retained profit for 1999	51	80
Profit and loss account balance 31 December 1998	282	202
Profit and loss account balance 31 December 1999	333	282

Balance Sheet at 31 December	1999	1998
Tangible Fixed Assets	*£000*	*£000*
Cost	5,220	3,600
Accumulated depreciation	2,360	1,700
	2,860	1,900
Current Assets	1,893	1,372
Creditors falling due within one year		
Loan repayment due	150	ýÿ
Other current liabilities including dividends and taxation	1,270	840
	1,420	840

Net current assets	473	532
Total assets less current liabilities	3,333	2,432
Creditorsýÿ Amounts falling due after more than one year		
10% Loan repayable 2000-2009	1,350	500
	1,983	1,932
Capital and Reserves		
Called up share capital		
(£1 ordinary shares)	1,400	1,400
Share premium account 250 250	250	250
Profit and loss account	333	282
	1,983	1,932

Note: Tamari raised a loan of £1 million during 1999; this together with the already existing loan is repayable by ten equal instalments over the period 2000-2009.

We can now apply some of the above ratios to the information provided for Tamari plc in Figure 1 together with the following information for 31 December 1997: fixed assets at cost, £2,700,000; current assets, £1,802,000; creditors falling due within one year, £838,000; called up share capital, £1,400,000. Cash flow per share (version 1), which is of limited interest in this case given Tamari's profit record, is not calculated below. Neither do we calculate CFAR because future forecasts are not provided. Cash flow from operations to current liabilities.

There has been a startling decline in this ratio between 1998 and 1999, falling to one half of the previous level. This has been caused by a combination of a reduction in the operating cash flow and a rise in average current liabilities. Nevertheless, the current liabilities (which include taxation and proposed dividends not payable until well into the year) remain adequately covered by cash flow on the assumption that this aspect of Tamari's financial affairs is repeated in the year 2000.

Cash recovery rate. The cash recovery rate has also fallen to about one half of the figure of the previous year. This implies that the company may now be recovering its investment in business assets over twice the period that was previously the case. It should be borne in mind, however, that the 1998 ratio benefited from the release of investment in working capital which was not, and probably could not, be repeated in 1999.

Cash flow per share (version II) and Capital expenditure per share. There is a small improvement in cash flow per share which shows that management is utilising more effectively the funds provided by equity shareholders in order to produce a surplus available for use in the business after all direct claims (interest, taxation and dividends) have been met.

The capital expenditure per share has risen dramatically and it is patently obvious that the company has had to look elsewhere to fund a much greater proportion of that investment in 1999 (115.7p 51.5p = 64.2p per share) compared with 1998 (64.3p - 50p = 14.3p per share).

DCSR. The DCSR for 1998 is strong, with EBITDA 6.8x the prospective interest charges for 1999; there is no loan repayment in that year. For 1999, the ratio declines to 3.9x but still shows debt commitments to be comfortably covered out of internally generated cash flow. The multiple also suggests that there is surplus cash available for working capital, capital expenditure, tax and dividend payments.

Ratios and percentages based entirely on the contents of the cash flow statement

Net cash flow from operating activities is given an index of 100 and becomes the pivotal figure for each of the other calculations. The presentation of calculations in Figure 2 is analogous to the expression of expenses in the profit and loss account as a percentage of sales.

Interest, taxation and dividends each absorbs a relatively small proportion of cash generated by Tamari from its business operations no more than 14.6% in any one case. In total, just 40.2% of internally generated funds are applied in financing the requirements of government and suppliers of long-term finance.

There has been a heavy investment in tangible fixed assets with 59.8% of the cash flow from operations (100% - 40.2%) used for this purpose. However, with the investment in fixed assets represented by an index of 148.4, the directors of Tamari have had to look elsewhere for the bulk of the funding.

These financial relationships may be contrasted with the previous year when the entire capital investment was funded from internal sources, and a significant proportion (24.2%) of cash flow from operating activities remained available to increase the cash balance.

The balance of long-term expenditure was entirely funded by the issue of a loan, leaving a small amount over to increase cash available at the end of 1999 compared with a year earlier.

It is possible to add to the interpretative value of the cash flow statement by expressing some of the financial totals in Figure 1 as ratios of one another. As is always the case with ratio analysis, the validity of a ratio depends on the existence of an expected relationship between the financial magnitudes being compared. A number of valid ratios could be computed and two are presented below as illustrative of the possibilities available.

The internal/external finance ratio. The relationship between internal and external finance may be examined by expressing profit before non-cash expenses as a ratio of external debt financing. A low ratio shows that the company is increasing its reliance on external funding, perhaps for the purpose of further investment, and a deterioration in the gearing position of the company would be likely to result. The calculations for Tamari are as follows:

1999

1998

Internal/external

finance ratio

1,161:1,000 =

1.2:1 1,020:100 =

10.2:1

We can see that Tamari placed very little increased reliance on external finance in 1998, but this has changed dramatically during 1999 with amounts generated internally and externally roughly equal. This will be reflected in a revision of the long-term capital structure of the company which could be interrogated further by computing leverage ratios based on the contents of the balance sheet.

2 The shareholder funding ratio. The extent to which the equity shareholders have funded business investment during the year can be examined by expressing free cash flow available to shareholders (cash flow after taxation, interest and dividends) as a percentage of expenditure on fixed assets and net current assets.

1999

1998

Shareholder funding ratio

721:1,689 = 0.43:1

700:310 = 2.3:1

The shareholders of Tamari comfortably funded the entire business investment in 1998, leaving a significant surplus to improve the companyýÿs liquidity position. In 1999, by way of contrast, the directors have decided to rely heavily on debt to fund the substantial investment programme undertaken during the year.

Conclusion

The purpose of the cash flow statement is to improve the informative value of published financial reports. The lack of prominence given to cash flow-based accounting ratios as a means of improving the interpretative value of this data is particularly surprising given the enormous amount of space usually devoted to traditional accounting ratios in text books on financial accounting, management accounting and corporate finance.

This article has demonstrated the contribution of three types of percentages and ratios: ratios to link the cash flow statement with key related items appearing in the balance sheet; the expression of each item in the cash flow statement as a percentage of net cash flow from operating activities; and the calculation of ratios to explore the inter-relationship between items within the cash flow statement.

As usual, it should be noted that different ratios are expressed in different ways, as percentages, as multiples, or in pence, as well as in the classic form.

The interpretative value of individual ratios will depend upon the nature of the financial developments at a particular business. Given the content of Figure 1, for example, the cash flow per share (version I) ratio was not seen to possess any interpretative value and was not calculated.

It is also the case that the messages conveyed by certain ratios may be similar for a particular company covering a particular year, but in a different time and place the same ratios may yield different insights.

Finally, one must remember the importance of not attaching too much weight to any single ratio but to use a representative range of ratios (including cash flow ratios!) to build up a meaningful business profile.

QUALIFIED AUDIT REPORTS

The purpose of this chapter is to explain the structure of the basic form of audit report and to describe the various forms of qualified audit reports and the situations which could lead to their use. Please note that for study purposes it is pointless trying to memorise the exact wording of these reports, instead concentrate upon the structure of the report and how this may change when a qualification is in prospect.

THE ELEMENTS OF AN AUDIT REPORT

These are as follows:

Title: the report is addressed to the members of the company, remember that the auditor is under a statutory duty to report to the members of the company.

Scope: The purpose of this paragraph is to ensure that the elements of the financial statements which are subject to audit are identified (by reference to the relevant page numbers in the annual report).This is important to avoid misunderstandings in relation to the auditor's opinion. An element of the so-called expectation gap which is claimed to exist between users of financial statements and auditors is the perception on the part of some users that the entire contents of the annual report are subject to audit so identifying the scope of the audit is crucial.

The following financial statements are subject to audit.

- The Balance Sheet.
- The Profit and Loss Account.
- The Cash Flow Statement.

- The Statement of Total Recognised Gains and Losses (STRGL).

Note that company law requires the first two of the above list to be audited whereas the auditor needs to audit the cash flow statement and STRGL because these have to be produced to comply with FRS1 and FRS3 respectively, and compliance with accounting standards is now an accepted part of achieving a true and fair view.

In addition, the auditors should disclose the details of directors remuneration and details of any transactions between a company and its directors or officers if the company has not given the required disclosures in the notes to its financial statements as required by company law.

Note that the auditor is also under a statutory duty to consider if:

- proper accounting records have been kept;
- the financial statements are in agreement with underlying records and returns;
- proper returns have been received from branches not visited by the auditor;
- adequate evidence and explanations have been made available to the auditor by the officers of the client;
- the directorsýÿ report is consistent with the financial statements.

Auditors use exception reporting in relation to the above duty, no reference to any of these matters in the audit report indicates that they have been considered and that the auditor is satisfied.

The basis of the opinion: The key point in this paragraph is that the audit is conducted in accordance with auditing standards, this gives a benchmark against which the quality of the audit may subsequently be judged in the event of any external scrutiny of the auditors work. Therefore it is very important that auditors can demonstrate compliance with ali relevant auditing standards in order to satisfy external scrutiny as a result of, for example, litigation against the auditor.

The opinion: The key parts of the opinion paragraph are that:

- the financial statements give a "true and fair view";
- the financial statements have been prepared in accordance with the Companies Act 1985.

In the event that the opinion is qualified the heading to the opinion paragraph will state "qualified opinion...."

Signature and date: The report must be signed by a registered auditor and dated. The date is significant because it specifies a key point in the post balance sheet events review period and it will usually be the same as the date of approval of the financial statements. The audit report cannot be dated before the date of approval because the financial statements do not legally exist until they have been approved by the directors.

QUALIFIED AUDIT REPORTS

It is necessary to firstly identify the circumstances which can give rise to a qualification.

These are as follows:

- Uncertainty arising from either a limitation upon the scope of the auditorsýÿ work or an inability to obtain any evidence regarding doubts which exist in relation to an unresolved matter.
- Disagreements arising from factual discrepancies, unsuitable accounting policies, inadequate or misleading disclosures given in the financial statements or failure to comply with an accounting

standard or legislation. Some of these types of disagreement should be resolved fairly easily with the client so that a qualification can be avoided, for example a factual disagreement should lead to the financial statements being amended to reflect the correct view. Other types of disagreement which are perhaps more subjective will be much more difficult to resolve such as those relating to the suitability of an accounting policy.

Secondly, it is necessary to decide upon the effect of the circumstances discussed above.

These are classified as:

- those having a material but not fundamental effect upon the financial statements;
- those having a fundamental effect upon the financial statements.

Fundamentalÿÿ means that the matter is such as to seriously distort or undermine the view which is given by the financial statements to the extent that they could mislead user groups.

The wording of the qualification can then be arrived at using one of the examples given in the appendix to SAS 600.

An except for qualification will be given when the matter is a material but not fundamental uncertainty or disagreement. An example of an uncertainty could be the destruction of a part of the clients accounting records leading to a limitation of scope being imposed upon the auditors work because audit evidence is then unavailable. An example of a disagreement under this heading could be a failure by a client to apply a reasonable depreciation policy to a particular class of fixed assets, however in both of these examples the effect is not pervasive to the view which the financial statements give as a whole.

An adverse opinion indicating that the financial statements do not give a true and fair view and/or do not comply with the Companies Act 1985 will be given when the matter concerned gives rise to a fundamental disagreement. An example of this could be that the client has failed to recognise a provision which would turn a reported profit into a loss and which would fundamentally change the net asset position if it were recognised. Such qualifications are relatively rare.

A disclaimer opinion will be given in the event of a fundamental uncertainty and the auditorsýÿ report will indicate that an opinion cannot be given. This a very unsatisfactory state of affairs for users and SAS 601 has been introduced to deal with the situation where the uncertainty arises because of an imposed limitation of scope by the directors. This is discussed later in the article.

Finally it is important to note that qualification only occurs in relation to material items.

INHERENT UNCERTAINTIES

Note that if there is an inherent uncertainty associated with the financial statements which the directors have disclosed to the best of their abilities in the notes to the accounts (and the auditors agree with the manner of disclosure) then an "explanatory paragraph" can be added to the "basis of opinion" section of the report to ensure that users attention is drawn to the matter concerned.

It is important to remember that this does not constitute an audit report qualification.

IMPOSED LIMITATION OF AUDIT SCOPE

This is a relatively recent standard which was designed to deal with the situation where the auditors response to a fundamental imposed limitation of scope placed upon their work, by the directors actions, is to simply issue a disclaimer type of report as described above.

In such situations the standard requires that:

- where it is apparent that the directors will impose a limitation before an assignment has been accepted, then the auditor should not accept the audit appointment;
- if an audit is accepted and then the auditor becomes aware of an imposed limitation (perhaps a refusal by the directors to provide key items of audit evidence) which is likely to result in a ÿÿdisclaimerÿÿ then the auditor should request the directors to remove the limitation and in the event it is not removed the auditor should resign. (Remember that the auditor has certain rights and duties under the Companies Act 1985 on resignation from office.)

CONCLUSION

Questions on audit reporting almost invariably involve a mini case study scenario where you are invited to comment upon the given circumstances and to discuss an appropriate type of auditors response. Make sure you understand the different types of circumstances which can lead to an audit report qualification and that you appreciate that the gravity of each circumstance can also affect the opinion.

2

Manage Organizational Costs and Optimize Profitability

Most successful organizations have a firm handle on revenue sources and direct costs. But many lack sufficient understanding of how the products they manufacture and the customers they serve consume support services and contribute to other indirect costs. Without detailed visibility into enterprise expenses for sales, distribution, finance, IT, and so forth, it's difficult to measure the financial performance of individual products and customers or make informed decisions that reduce costs and optimize profitability.

Activity-based costing (ABC) has long been recognized as a valuable tool for managing costs and improving performance. When conducted effectively, ABC provides rich insight into enterprise performance and action-oriented information that help managers at any level of the organization use this data as a baseline for strategy development.

EMPOWER MANAGER AND EXECUTIVE DECISION MAKING

With the Business Objects Profitability and Cost Management application from Business Objects, an SAP company, organizations like yours – in industries from financial services to the public sector – can increase visibility into enterprise costs. The application helps you align operational resources and capacity with demand. You can thereby increase revenues by focusing on multiple dimensions of your business, including the products, customers, and distribution channels that are most profitable.

The application enables user-friendly, rapid, and efficient modeling. It is a scalable, enterprise-class application that meets business needs from local and regional to global.

With reliable, on-demand analysis and scenario modeling, you have deeper insight into the levers affecting costs and profitability at any time. Activity-centric functionality extends the value of profitability and cost management activities.

And BusinessObjects Profitability and Cost Management integrates with both SAP and non-SAP solutions for sophisticated, seamless analysis. With comprehensive ABC functionality, the SAP solution provides additional value over and above traditional ABC solutions.

RELIABLE, ON-DEMAND WHAT-IF ANALYSIS AND SCENARIO MODELING

Having the right information when you need it is critical to making smart, timely business decisions. BusinessObjects Profitability and Cost Management puts valuable data at the fingertips of users across the enterprise, enabling your organization to operate with agility and flexibility.

You can model costs at any level in the organization, down to highly granular transaction data. Instead of relying on batch updates and other slow, inefficient methods, you have competitive advantage with on-demand reporting and analysis.

BusinessObjects Profitability and Cost Management will help identify areas for cost improvements, such as instances of waste or high-cost activities, and facilitate proactive decision making to rectify problems.

USER-FRIENDLY, RAPID, AND EFFICIENT MODELING

BusinessObjects Profitability and Cost Management enables visibility into the drivers of cost and profitability with activity-centric, multidimensional modeling and analysis functionality.

Employees can build even complex ABC models easily with an intuitive, user-friendly interface and predefined dimensions then quickly distribute to enterprise users. Create agile, adaptable analytical models that truly reflect organizational costs and that can be easily maintained, updated, and altered to meet changing business circumstances. The application minimizes the need for external consultants and significant manual maintenance, reducing your total cost of ownership and improving your technology ROI. Powerful functionality enables you to do the following:

- Build models rapidly with a user-friendly interface with "point-and-click" default assignments and reassignments in a predefined multidimensional structure offering unlimited attributes
- Model complex situations across multiple periods and versions with an adaptable rules engine
- Support comprehensive ABC methodologies, including time-split and time-driven costing, with a wizard for writing time equations and calculating other drivers
- Maintain models with minimal effort
- Integrate with Microsoft Office and other third-party reporting and analysis tools

A SCALABLE, ENTERPRISE-CLASS SOLUTION

BusinessObjects Profitability and Cost Management is a Web-based application that is scalable to meet business requirements ranging from single-site implementations to global deployments. In addition to scalability, the solution is flexible to meet the complexity of your analytical requirements.

Perform simple analyses or model complex, high-volume ABC activities with a combination of multidimensional and relational data structures – without compromising accuracy. And you can leverage existing Web infrastructure to deploy the solution across the enterprise for easy, fast, and cost-effective implementation. What's more, you can do the following:

- Optimize nonsystem-data collection and reporting for local and remote users with unique Web-based forms and integrated work-management functionality
- Speed remote deployment, minimize training, accelerate user adoption, and increase productivity through Web-based data entry and reporting
- Integrate with global offices using multicurrency and multilingual functionality
- Facilitate configuration and enterprise security and access processes with time-and date-stamped audit-trail functionality
- Eliminate need for local models distributed throughout the organization with centralized model administration and maintenance over the Web
- Export multiple-level results to third-party databases and enable high-volume account and transactional processing

BusinessObjects Profitability and Cost Management is a Web-based application that is scalable to meet business requirements ranging from single-site implementations to global deployments

Improve organizational understanding of how customers contribute to fixed costs – and make more precise decisions on how to grow the business, reengineer products, or reeducate customers on purchasing activities. For example, by having a customer place monthly instead of weekly orders, you can cut costs from the order-to-cash process, saving money for both of you.

Boost user confidence in the accuracy and integrity of ABC results. Enable employees to translate good ideas into action – fast – with collaborative tools, what-if analytical functionality, and the ability to easily update and share models in real time. BusinessObjects Profit-ability and Cost Management enables you to:

- Slice and dice data and analysis results, create charts, drill down from summary views to detailed cost data, and link to related budgeting and metrics models
- Perform on-demand queries and what-if analysis on reliable, Web-accessible data, testing out the financial impact of assumptions before committing to them
- Maintain data in a central repository for greater efficiency and control over critical business information

EXTEND THE VALUE OF PROFITABILITY AND COST MANAGEMENT

BusinessObjects Profitability and Cost Management enables activity-centric performance management in a single application, with functionality that goes beyond costing and profitability reporting. The application facilitates services costing and cross-charging, as well as driver-based and activity-based planning and budgeting. You can do the following:

- Accurately cross-charge IT and other shared services with predefined dimensions and reiterative reallocation functionality
- Improve transparency with detailed invoices that help users make decisions on shared-services consumption
- Provide essential data to better align shared-services resources with demand and make shared-services departments more efficient and more accountable to the enterprise
- Gain insight into dimensions including the cost and profitability of products, services, customers, and channels for creating planning and budgeting models
- Deliver activity-based planning and budgeting models by changing driver volumes and "back calculating" existing ABC models
- Gain a more iterative understanding of what drives organizational costs with driver-based models
- Rapidly reforecast by updating driver data and aligning operational capacity with demand

SAP SOLUTIONS FOR ENTERPRISE PERFORMANCE MANAGEMENT

BusinessObjects Profitability and Cost Management is part of the SAP solutions for enterprise performance management – a comprehensive set of solutions that help your company capitalize on the value of your existing data assets. With these solutions, your organization becomes more agile, gaining organizational alignment, visibility, and greater confidence to give you optimal control and competitive advantage.

These solutions can work with SAP Business Suite applications; SAP solutions for governance, risk, and compliance; and the business intelligence platform from SAP. As a result you can maximize business profitability, manage risk and compliance, and optimize corporate systems, people, and processes.

SUMMARY

Gain a deep understanding of the levers affecting organizational costs and profitability with the BusinessObjects Profitability and Cost Management application. Identify underlying causes of underperformance, test potential impacts of changes, and take incisive action to reduce costs and optimize profitability of products, customers, and channels.

CHALLENGES

- Limited visibility into cost and profitability details and dimensions
- Inefficient cost reporting that fails to provide insights for improving financial performance
- Lack of transparency into cross-charges and insufficient insight into cost of support services
- Annual budgets that are disconnected from operational reality

SUPPORTED BUSINESS PROCESSES AND SOFTWARE FUNCTIONS

- Activity-based costing for informed management decisions that optimize customer and product profitability, reduce the cost to serve, and optimize cost of key processes
- Shared-services costing and cross-charging to align resources and capacities with demand, reduce delivery costs, and gain process transparency
- On-demand, what-if scenario analysis; driver-based and activity-based budgeting

- Dynamic monitoring of the drivers of cost and profitability

Business Benefits

- Visibility into the true drivers impacting costs and profitability, including IT shared services, via a user-friendly interface
- Optimized costs and profitability thanks to a detailed understanding of multidimensional drivers such as product, service, customer, and channel
- Alignment by matching of operational capacity and support functions with demand for flawless execution of strategy
- Incisive decision making due to rapid identification of underlying causes of changes in organizational cost and profitability, with the capability to test the impact of potential adjustments

HOW TO MANAGE RISING CONSTRUCTION COSTS

Everyone in the industry has become concerned over the last few years about the rapid escalation of construction costs.

According to *Engineering News-Record*, the Construction Cost Index (CCI) posted a gain of 4.6 percent last year. The Building Cost Index (BCI) showed an increase of 5 percent for the year, mostly due to higher steel prices. The Materials Cost Index (MCI) ended the year with a 6.4 percent increase, as material price escalation provided the most fuel for inflation.

Some experts predict these numbers may level off somewhat this year due to record levels in the housing market and a potential slowdown in China's economy. But even if these optimistic forecasts are accurate, they would simply bring construction costs back in line with typical inflation numbers. The biggest driver of construction costs is the price of materials.

Over the last 18 months, steel prices skyrocketed more than 50 percent. Much of this was because of increased demand from China (two-thirds of the world's construction projects are underway in South China) as well as reduced exports from Russia, the Ukraine, and other major producers. This price inflation led to a ripple effect in the industry—from structural steel to metal studs. Builders who signed fixed-price contracts were forced to pass their costs along to developers. Others hedge by guaranteeing prices for a short time only.

This year's most troublesome hot spots are forecast to be oil-, plastic-, and copper-based products. All are expected to remain volatile throughout the rest of the year.

Fortunately, the design-build process gives owners many opportunities to manage the unpredictability of rising materials cost. The design-build process enables a single responsible party to manage costs from the project conception to completion. Cost-saving decisions can be made early in the process through value engineering and value management.

On a recent redevelopment project, a 450-car parking garage had a preliminary design calling for structural steel and cast-in-place concrete. The Bannett Group (a company of which I am the president) reengineered the project to a precast structure, allowing the parking garage to come in under budget despite the escalating steel cost.

One of the greatest advantages in the design-build process is the ability to fast-track so that the project can go from conception to completion in record time. Fast-tracking provides the ability to close vendor contracts at an early stage to lock in the lowest possible price. On a recent retail project in the South Jersey region, we avoided cost increases by developing the steel design and locking in the pricing more than six months ahead of schedule.

Through the design-build process, we can identify the quantity of steel, masonry, and other needed materials from our earliest conceptual designs. We can then work with suppliers to order materials at the beginning of the process, thereby locking in the lowest possible price. Suppliers will hold their prices with an order so we can provide a guaranteed maximum price to our clients.

We also believe in incorporating the value-engineering process during the design phase, so we can make decisions in a timely manner to help control costs.

For example, depending on the market, it may be advantageous to use wood rather than steel or masonry. Load-bearing walls may be more cost-effective than steel columns during a period of volatile steel pricing. On several recent retail projects, The Bannett Group design team changed the structure to load-bearing walls to maintain the budget.

In the design-build process, decisions made in the early stages of design have minimal cost impact on the project. Design-build creates a guaranteed maximum price and eliminates change orders during the construction phase, when they cost considerably more than they would during the design process.

The bottom line is this: Single-source responsibility saves time and money by expediting the process. With careful planning, spiraling construction costs can be controlled.

How To: Plan for the rising cost of construction materials Costs for copper, gypsum and other materials have skyrocketed; make sure you're prepared for escalating construction costs before starting your project.

Once upon a time, contractors gave construction project estimates that were good for weeks, and owners could take their time negotiating contracts.

But today, demand from China and India, the Hurricane Katrina rebuilding effort, high new home construction rates and speculation in the commodity markets are driving prices for copper, gypsum and other building materials to unprecedented heights and adding an unwelcome complexity to construction projects from conception to completion.

The price pressures have left local construction companies scrambling to manage costs without sacrificing quality, said John D. Pumper, chief financial officer for Garfield Heights-based D-A-S Construction Co.

> *"There are a lot of things outside of our borders affecting things inside our borders that we have no control over," Mr. Pumper said. "It certainly has me concerned ... how we are going to be able to continue working for our clients to build their projects for them at a price that they can afford."*

The reality is that current price trends are going to require owners to spend more money — 10% to 15% more— to get the same project done, Mr. Pumper said. Prices for gypsum, which is used to make drywall and plaster, leapt 26% from May 2005 to May 2006 as residential home construction pushed plants to full capacity, said Jim Haughey, chief economist at Reed Construction Data, a research firm based in Norcross, Ga. The price that electricians and plumbers pay for copper has doubled due to a high level of construction and speculation in the financial markets, he said.

In addition, prices for cement and petroleum-based products like asphalt roofing installation are on the rise.

Facing the Facts

Barry Miller, a partner with the law firm Benesch, Friedlander, Coplan & Aronoff LLP in Cleveland, said property owners must acknowledge this new market reality of "dramatic and unpredictable price escalation" and its far-reaching implications. The price volatility characterizing today's construction materials market has adversely affected the accuracy of pre-construction estimates, shortened the timeframe for contract negotiation and even hindered some contractors' ability to complete projects, he said.

Those who don't educate themselves and take action to manage construction costs risk spending beyond their budgets or, worse, enduring financial collapse, Mr. Miller said.

He advises owners to plan for the worst-case scenario by increasing the size of contingency costs in their budget to account for rising material costs and putting performance bonds in place to protect themselves if a contractor is unable to complete the project.

Performance bonds are three-party instruments between a surety, contractor and owner in which a bonding company assumes the risk and agrees to fulfill the contractor's obligations by providing funds or hiring replacements if needed. The risk management mechanisms increase project costs, but are well worth it when doubt exists about a contractor's ability to get the job done, Mr. Miller said.

"You (the owner) may be doing everything right, but in certain situations you have a contractor who doesn't have the financial resources to weather the storm," he said.

Banks providing project financing also look favorably upon bonding and contractor insurance policies like Subguard, a bonding alternative that gives contractors more control in the face of default than traditional performance bonds, said David Drummond, national construction engineering manager at KeyBank.

Additionally, the current price environment has prompted banks to add more contingency funds — 5% to 8% compared with 3% to 5% in the past — to construction loans and to be more selective about their borrowers, he said.

"We're looking at best-in-class developers that can bring things to market in budget and on schedule," Mr. Drummond said. And in the event that things still go south, banks work to renegotiate loan terms, find equity partners to infuse cash into the deal, finance a mezzanine loan or increase the loan amount where appropriate, he said.

"It doesn't make sense for us to stop funding unless it is a huge problem," Mr. Drummond said.

"We like to work with developers to come to a successful conclusion."

Sharing the Burden

Contractors say that the recent wave of market volatility has made closer relationships with architects, owners and other industry participants indispensable.

It is important that all parties stay attuned to the market and in communication with each other so that expectations are realistic, said Don Dreier, executive vice president for Donley's Inc., a Cleveland-based construction firm.

"The biggest thing we continue to do is stay in touch with suppliers, vendors and economists, who look at these (material price) trends, so that as we prepare estimates we're using the most current information available," he said. Publications such as Engineering News-Record, a trade journal, also are valuable resources, he said. "We are constantly trying to educate the owners of what's going on in the marketplace so that the pricing that we're giving them is not overly escalated, but they are sharing in the risk if pricing does increase sharply, " he said.

Current market conditions have made fair price escalator clauses —contract provisions that distribute price increase burden between contractors and owners — more popular, Mr. Miller said.

Typically, the burden of swelling prices rests on contractors' shoulders so they pad price quotations to shield themselves from fluctuations.

"They add a factor to their pricing to account for the fact that they are going to have to pay more when the time comes to place the order," Mr. Miller said. "If dramatic increase doesn't occur, the windfall goes to the contractor."

By contrast, fair price escalator clauses eliminate hidden contractor contingencies and state that the owner will cover price increases based on an agreed upon material price index.

Managing Costs

Owners also may buy construction materials for themselves at a project's outset to avoid the price increases that can occur during the long timeframe between contractor bidding and material ordering.

Pre-purchasing materials "is an alternative that people can utilize to minimize price uncertainty," Mr. Miller said. But it's not for everyone and is most appropriate for experienced owners with the means to accurately identify the amount of materials needed and key supplier relationships, he said. Getting the contractor involved on the front lines with the architect also can help manage construction costs.

This type of designer-builder collaboration is a dramatic departure from the typical procedure where multiple contractors bid on projects designed without their input, but leads to smarter and more cost-effective solutions for the owner, said Mr. Pumper of D-A-S Construction.

He has found that when contractors are engaged earlier in the process, they can work with the architect to find savings at each project level from more cost-effective design to alternative materials that accomplish the same thing. "There's not one silver bullet as a part of this project," Mr. Pumper said. "It is accomplishing a lot of little things that add up to big savings for our clients."

Cost Estimators

- Nature of the Work
- Training, Other Qualifications, and Advancement
- Employment
- Job Outlook
- Projections Data
- Earnings
- OES Data
- Related Occupations
- Sources of Additional Information

SIGNIFICANT POINTS

About 62 percent of cost estimators work in the construction industry, and another 15 percent are employed in manufacturing industries.

Voluntary certification can be valuable to cost estimators; some individual employers may require professional certification for employment.

Very good employment opportunities are expected.

In construction and manufacturing, job prospects should be best for those with industry work experience and a bachelor's degree in a related field.

NATURE OF THE WORK

Accurately forecasting the scope, cost, and duration of future projects is vital to the survival of any business. Cost estimators develop the cost information that business owners or managers need to make a bid for a contract or to decide on the profitability of a proposed new product or project. They also determine which endeavors are making a profit.

Regardless of the industry in which they work, estimators compile and analyze data on all of the factors that can influence costs, such as materials, labor, location, duration of the project, and special machinery requirements, including computer hardware and software. Job duties vary widely depending on the type and size of the project.

The methods for estimating costs can differ greatly by industry. On a construction project, for example, the estimating process begins with the decision to submit a bid. After reviewing various preliminary drawings and specifications, the estimator visits the site of the proposed project.

The estimator needs to gather information on access to the site; the availability of electricity, water, and other services; and surface topography and drainage. The estimator usually records this information in a signed report that is included in the final project estimate.

After the site visit, the estimator determines the quantity of materials and labor the firm will need to furnish. This process, called the quantity survey or "takeoff," involves completing standard estimating forms, filling in dimensions, numbers of units, and other information. A cost estimator working for a general contractor, for example, estimates the costs of all of the items that the contractor must provide. Although subcontractors estimate their costs as part of their own bidding process, the general contractor's cost estimator often analyzes bids made by subcontractors. Also during the takeoff process, the estimator must make decisions concerning equipment needs, the sequence of operations, the size of the crew required, and physical constraints at the site.

Allowances for wasted materials, inclement weather, shipping delays, and other factors that may increase costs also must be incorporated in the estimate.

After completing the quantity surveys, the estimator prepares a cost summary for the entire project, including the costs of labor, equipment, materials, subcontracts, overhead, taxes, insurance, markup, and any other costs that may affect the project. The chief estimator then prepares the bid proposal for submission to the owner.

Construction cost estimators also may be employed by the project's architect or owner to estimate costs or to track actual costs relative to bid specifications as the project develops. Estimators often specialize in large construction companies employing more than one estimator. For example, one may estimate only electrical work and another may concentrate on excavation, concrete, and forms.

In manufacturing and other firms, cost estimators usually are assigned to the engineering, cost, or pricing department. The estimator's goal is to accurately estimate the costs associated with making products.

The job may begin when management requests an estimate of the costs associated with a major redesign of an existing product or the development of a new product or production process. When estimating the cost of developing a new product, for example, the estimator works with engineers, first reviewing blueprints or conceptual drawings to determine the machining operations, tools, gauges, and materials that would be required.

The estimator then prepares a parts list and determines whether it is more efficient to produce or to purchase the parts. To do this, the estimator asks for price information from potential suppliers.

The next step is to determine the cost of manufacturing each component of the product. Some high-technology products require a considerable amount of computer programming during the design phase. The cost of software development is one of the fastest growing and most difficult activities to estimate. As a result, some cost estimators now specialize in estimating only computer software development and related costs.

The cost estimator then prepares time-phase charts and learning curves. Time-phase charts indicate the time required for tool design and fabrication, tool "debugging"—finding and correcting all problems—manufacturing of parts, assembly, and testing.

Learning curves graphically represent the rate at which the performance of workers producing parts for the new product improves with practice. These curves are commonly called "cost reduction" curves, because many problems—such as engineering changes, rework, shortages of parts, and lack of operator skills—diminish as the number of units produced increases, resulting in lower unit costs.

Using all of this information, the estimator then calculates the standard labor hours necessary to produce a specified number of units. Standard labor hours are then converted to dollar values, to which are added factors for waste, overhead, and profit to yield the unit cost in dollars. The estimator then compares the cost of purchasing parts with the firm's estimated cost of manufacturing them to determine which is cheaper.

Computers play an integral role in cost estimation because estimating often involves complex mathematical calculations and requires advanced mathematical techniques. For example, to undertake a parametric analysis (a process used to estimate costs per unit based on square footage or other specific requirements of a project), cost estimators use a computer database containing information on the costs and conditions of many other similar projects. Although computers cannot be used for the entire estimating process, they can relieve estimators of much of the drudgery associated with routine, repetitive, and time-consuming calculations. New and improved cost estimating software has lead to more efficient computations, leaving estimators greater time to visit and analyze projects.

Operations research, production control, cost, and price analysts who work for government agencies may do significant amounts of cost estimating in the course of their regular duties. In addition, the duties of construction managers may include estimating costs. (For more information, see the statements on operations research analysts and construction managers elsewhere in the *Handbook*.)

Although estimators spend most of their time in a comfortable office, construction estimators also visit worksites that can be dusty, dirty, and occasionally hazardous. Likewise, estimators in manufacturing spend time on the factory floor, where it also can be noisy and dirty. In some industries, frequent travel between a firm's headquarters and its subsidiaries or subcontractors may be required.

Estimators normally work a 40-hour week, but overtime is common. Cost estimators often work under pressure and stress, especially when facing bid deadlines. Inaccurate estimating can cause a firm to lose a bid or to lose money on a job that was not accurately estimated.

TRAINING, OTHER QUALIFICATIONS, AND ADVANCEMENT

Job entry requirements for cost estimators vary by industry. In the construction industry, employers increasingly prefer to hire cost estimators with a bachelor's degree in construction science, construction management, or building science, although it is also possible for experienced construction workers to become cost estimators. Employers in manufacturing usually prefer someone with a bachelor's degree in mathematics, statistics, or engineering.

Education and training. In the construction industry, employers increasingly prefer individuals with a degree in building science, construction management, or construction science, all of which usually include several courses in cost estimating. Most construction estimators also have considerable construction experience, gained through work in the industry, internships, or cooperative education programs. Applicants with a thorough knowledge of construction materials, costs, and procedures in areas ranging from heavy construction to electrical work, plumbing systems, or masonry work have a competitive edge.

In manufacturing industries, employers prefer to hire individuals with a degree in engineering, physical science, operations research, mathematics, or statistics or in accounting, finance, business, economics, or a related subject. In most industries, experience in quantitative techniques is important.

Many colleges and universities include cost estimating as part of bachelor's and associate degree curriculums in civil engineering, industrial engineering, and construction management or construction engineering technology. In addition, cost estimating is often part of master's degree programs in construction science or construction management.

Organizations representing cost estimators, such as the Association for the Advancement of Cost Engineering (AACE International) and the Society of Cost Estimating and Analysis (SCEA), also sponsor educational and professional development programs. These programs help students, estimators-in-training, and experienced estimators learn about changes affecting the profession. Specialized courses and programs in cost-estimating techniques and procedures also are offered by many technical schools, community colleges, and universities.

Estimators also receive much training on the job because every company has its own way of handling estimates. Working with an experienced estimator, newcomers become familiar with each step in the process. Those with no experience reading construction specifications or blueprints first learn that aspect of the work.

Then they may accompany an experienced estimator to the construction site or shop floor, where they observe the work being done, take measurements, or perform other routine tasks. As they become more knowledgeable, estimators learn how to tabulate quantities and dimensions from drawings and how to select the appropriate prices for materials.

Other qualifications. Cost estimators should have an aptitude for mathematics; be able to quickly analyze, compare, and interpret detailed but sometimes poorly defined information; and be able to make sound and accurate judgments based on this information. The ability to focus on details, while analyzing and overcoming larger obstacles, is essential. Assertiveness and self-confidence in presenting and supporting conclusions are also important, as are strong communications and interpersonal skills, because estimators may work as part of a team alongside managers, owners, engineers, and design professionals. Cost estimators also need knowledge of computers, including word-processing and spreadsheet packages. In some instances, familiarity with special estimation software or programming skills also may be required.

Certification and advancement. Voluntary certification can be valuable to cost estimators because it provides professional recognition of the estimator's competence and experience. In some instances, individual employers may even require professional certification for employment.

Both AACE International and SCEA administer certification programs. To become certified, estimators usually must have between 2 and 8 years of estimating experience and must pass an examination. In addition, certification requirements may include the publication of at least one article or paper in the field.

For most estimators, advancement takes the form of higher pay and prestige. Some move into management positions, such as project manager for a construction firm or manager of the industrial engineering department for a manufacturer. Others may go into business for themselves as consultants, providing estimating services for a fee to government or to construction or manufacturing firms.

EMPLOYMENT

Cost estimators held about 221,000 jobs in 2006. About 62 percent of estimators were in the construction industry, and another 15 percent were employed in manufacturing. The remainder worked in a wide range of other industries.

Cost estimators work throughout the country, usually in or near major industrial, commercial, and government centers and in cities and suburban areas undergoing rapid change or development.

JOB OUTLOOK

Employment of cost estimators is expected to grow faster than average. Very good employment opportunities are expected.

Employment change. Employment is expected to grow by 19 percent between 2006 and 2016, which is faster than the average for all occupations. Employment growth in the construction industry, in which most cost estimators are employed, will account for the majority of new jobs in this occupation.

Construction and repair of highways, streets, bridges, subway systems, airports, water and sewage systems, and electric power plants and transmission lines will stimulate demand for many more cost estimators.

Similarly, increasing population and business growth will result in more construction of residential homes, office buildings, shopping malls, hospitals, schools, restaurants, and other structures that require cost estimators. As the population ages, the demand for nursing and extended-care facilities will also increase. The growing complexity of construction projects will also boost demand for cost estimators as a larger number of workers specialize in a particular area of construction.

Job prospects. Because there are no formal bachelor's degree programs in cost estimating, some employers have difficulty recruiting qualified cost estimators, resulting in very good employment opportunities. Job prospects in construction should be best for those who have a degree in construction science, construction management, or building science plus practical experience in the various phases of construction or in a specialty craft area. For cost estimating jobs in manufacturing, those with degrees in mathematics, statistics, engineering, accounting, business administration, or economics should have the best job prospects.

In addition to job openings arising from employment growth, many additional openings should result annually from the need to replace workers who transfer to other occupations due to the sometimes stressful nature of the work, or who retire or leave the occupation for other reasons.

Employment of cost estimators, like that of many other construction workers, is sensitive to the fluctuations of the economy. Workers in these trades may experience periods of unemployment when the overall level of construction falls. On the other hand, shortages of these workers may occur in some areas during peak periods of building activity.

CONSTRUCTION COST

Article 64.-Principles for Elaborating Construct Cost Estimates

1. Projects using State-budget capital, State guaranteed capital and/or development investment credit capital must draw up all documents on estimate of necessary cost of the construction work.
2. The investor and the consultancy organization shall have to base themselves on the State's regulations on management of construction costs to elaborate and submit to the competent person for ratification the total cost estimate and construction item cost estimates, which shall serve as basis for organizing the construction and installation bidding and the cost management after the bidding.
3. The construction and installation contractor shall base on the State's regulations on management of

construction costs as reference when elaborating the price offered in the bid for construction works.

Article 65.-Management of Construction Costs

1. The State shall manage the construction costs through the promulgation of regimes and policies, principles and methods for elaborating unit prices and estimates; technical and economic norms; norms for investment and construction consultancy expenses; the investment capital ratio so as to determine the total investment of the project, the total cost estimate, the construction cost estimate.
2. The Ministry of Construction shall, together with the concerned ministries and State management bodies at different levels, have to manage the construction costs, based on the above-mentioned principles.
3. The provincial/municipal Construction Services shall work together with concerned bodies in elaborating the construction unit prices in their respective localities and submit them to the provincial level People's Committee for promulgation and application to the construction works of the State or State enterprises in the provinces and cities.
4. The Ministry of Construction shall guide the elaboration and management of construction costs.

Article 66.-The total Cost Estimate, Construct Item Cost Estimates

1. The total project cost estimate shall serve as basis for the management of construction costs, including costs of surveying, designing, construction and installation, equipment procurement, land use, compensation for ground clearance, resettlement of population, construction work insurance premiums,

taxes, other expenses including those for relevant scientific and technological studies with regard to Group A projects and a number of other projects with special requirements, permitted by the persons competent to decide the investment, and 10% reserve expense (including inflation rate and newly arising volume).

2. For construction and investment projects of State enterprises, the construction cost in all forms of bidding, bidder designation or self-execution must not exceed the total construction cost estimate of construction item cost estimates, which have already been ratified. Where due to force majeure reasons, the arising cost exceeds the ratified total construction cost estimate or construction item cost estimate, the appraisal thereof must be conducted and reported to the persons competent to decide the investment for consideration and decision.

CONSTRUCTION COST ESTIMATES

To adequately define the project scope and budget, cost estimates are required during the various stages of project development. As the project progresses, the estimates are refined to verify that the project is still cost effective, sufficient funds are available for construction, and the Contractor's bid price is reasonable. This Chapter discusses the various project estimates that are required and who is responsible for their preparation.

PROGRAMMING ESTIMATES

Bridge Replacement Projects

For bridge replacement projects, cost estimates are generally provided at the following stages of project development:

1. Program Action Request (PAR). The Project Manager is responsible for determining the construction cost estimate at this stage of project development. The cost estimate typically is developed based on the area of the proposed bridge deck (ft2), the type of structure (e.g., steel, concrete), recent similar projects in the geographic area, and engineering judgment. This estimate is completed before the Preliminary Bridge Plans are prepared; however, it should include all project elements from all units including road items, traffic items, etc. Include this cost estimate with the PAR.
2. Project Planning Report (PPR). The Project Manager is responsible for updating the cost estimate determined for the PAR at this stage of project development. This estimate is prepared in a similar manner as for the PAR. Include this estimate with the PPR.
3. Engineer's Estimate. The Engineer's Estimate is a very detailed construction cost estimate developed from final computed quantities and the appropriate unit costs.

Other Projects

Through various stages of project development, the Bridge Design Section will be responsible for providing the appropriate Project Manager with a cost estimate of the structural elements included in a road design project.

Additional Costs

In addition to the costs developed for the structure and approach roadways, the following will apply:

1. Preliminary Engineering. Preliminary engineering costs are generally calculated to be between 10% and

15% of the construction cost estimate. This percentage may be adjusted upwards for projects that require a considerable effort relative to the amount of construction involved, or the percentage could be less for projects that do not require as much time and effort for studies and plan preparation.

2. Utilities. The Utilities Office will provide the utilities relocation cost estimate.
3. Right-of-Way. The Right of Way Office will provide all right-of-way costs. Right-of-way costs are initially calculated using an estimated acreage and the number of relocations denoted during the scoping review. The estimates should include an appropriate percentage increase to cover personnel services and equipment, appraisals, condemnation settlements, and other miscellaneous costs that are difficult to anticipate during the initial stages of project development.
4. Traffic Control. The Traffic Engineering Division will provide a cost estimate for traffic control.
5. Construction Engineering and Contingencies Costs. After the construction cost estimate has been determined, 10% to 15% is added for engineering and contingencies costs.
6. Project Scope Changes. If the project scope changes or if the project cost significantly increases at any point during the planning or design process, the Project Manager will notify the State Bridge Design Engineer.

ENGINEER'S ESTIMATE

The Engineer's Estimate provides the Department with a basis for evaluating the bids for bridge and highway construction and allows the Department to determine if the low bid price is fair and reasonable for the work involved. This Estimate, plus the data used to generate the Estimate, is considered confidential and is not for general distribution. This Section discusses the procedures for developing this cost estimate.

Engineer's Estimates for all Department projects (e.g., bridge projects, road improvements, safety improvements) are forwarded to the Specifications and Estimate Group in the Road Design Section.

Responsibilities

Design Units

The following discusses the responsibilities of the various units for the preparation of the Engineer's Estimate:

1. Bridge Design Section. The Bridge Design Teams are responsible for entering all quantities into the Department's estimating software package (i.e., Transport's Proposal and Estimates System (PES)). The Bridge Design Teams are responsible for providing the Bridge Cost Estimate Coordinator with a set of plans for the project and any information that may influence the cost of the project (e.g., special commitments, experimental materials, special equipment, expected construction delays). Other Department Sections and Divisions will prepare their own cost estimates (e.g., Utilities, Traffic).
2. Road Design Section. The Road Design Groups are responsible for providing the Specifications and Estimate Group with a complete set of quantities and plans for the road design portion of the project.
3. Utilities Office. The Utilities Office will provide the Specifications and Estimate Group with completed costs and specifications for any utilities work to be included in the contract.

4. Traffic Engineering Division. The various Sections within the Traffic Engineering Division (e.g., Signing, Traffic Signals, Highway Lighting, Pavement Markings) are responsible for supplying the Specifications and Estimate Group with a complete cost estimate for their applicable design work for direct incorporation into the Engineer's Estimate.
5. Changes. If an estimated quantity or pay item is changed, the Bridge Design Team should immediately notify the Bridge Cost Estimate Coordinator of the change. The Bridge Cost Estimate Coordinator will revise the estimate accordingly.

Bridge Cost Estimate Coordinator

The Bridge Cost Estimate Coordinator will develop the Engineer's Estimate for in-house-designed bridge projects.

Consultants

The Consultant is responsible for preparing the Engineer's Estimate for Consultant-designed projects. The Project Manager is responsible for reviewing the cost estimate and forwarding it to the Bridge Cost Estimate Coordinator for review.

Computer Programs

Transport is AASHTO's information system for managing transportation programs, beginning with planning and estimating, and continuing through to the development of bidding documents, letting and contract award, and management of construction operations. Transport also provides a database of historical costs.

The Department uses two modules from the AASHTO Transport software program to track cost estimates. These programs are described below:

1. PES. The Transport Proposal and Estimates System (PES) is an interactive, online system for managing project information during the pre-letting phase of a construction project. PES permits the flexible definition of a project and its associated funding requirements to track and manage project cost information and set up the bidding proposal prior to the bid letting activity.

   With PES, data can be entered at the project, category, and item level. Grouping of multiple projects is allowed to track all related costs and funding sources. PES supports the preparation of the PS&E for Federal-aid bridge construction projects and allows projects to be combined into proposals for bid letting. The Bridge Design Section is responsible for entering the required data into PES for in-house-designed bridge projects, and the Project Manager is responsible for entering the required data into PES for Consultant-designed projects.

2. LAS. The Transport Letting and Award System (LAS) provides the capabilities to automate the many tasks that are necessary during the letting and award stages of a transportation construction project. LAS aids in advertising bids, tracking plan and proposal holders, processing bid information, evaluating bids, and making award decisions. It provides online and batch data entry with full edit checking and verification for vendor bids, produces the bid tabulation report, and performs analyses on received bids. LAS also maintains the Planholder's List, produces mailing lists, and maintains information for invoicing vendors for proposals and plans purchased.

Estimating Guidelines

The estimator should consider the following:

1. Historical Data. The Bridge Cost Estimate Coordinator maintains a database with unit prices on similar projects in similar geographic areas allowing the estimator to compile cost data for like structural elements and construction costs.
2. Unit Costs. Based on the proposed scope for the project, the estimator may revise unit prices based on the following factors:
   - geographic location (e.g., urban/rural, engineering district);
   - similarity to recent bridge projects;
   - inflation (adjustments to past prices to reflect the current year);
   - reliability of recent construction cost data;
   - recent trends in cost of materials, labor, and equipment;
   - anticipated difficulty of construction;
   - project size relative to size of similar projects;
   - proposed project schedule;
   - anticipated construction staging;
   - expected environmental problems (e.g., hazardous wastes, wetlands);
   - use of experimental materials; and
   - engineering judgment.
3. Lump-Sum Items. Desirably, lump-sum items should not be used on a project. However, this is not always practical. In determining the unit price for lump-sum items, the estimator should consider the following:

a. Components. Most lump-sum items can be divided into individual parts for estimating purposes. Once the elements have been tabulated, the estimator should use engineering judgment to determine the appropriate cost for each component.

The following are some example components of a bridge project:

- Structural Steel. Base the cost of the steel for the structure on the weight of the steel.
- Drainage System. Calculate the cost of the drainage system by determining the number of drains plus the total length of pipe required for the project.
- Utility PVC Conduit. Calculate the cost of PVC conduit by the length of the conduit used for the project. When the PVC conduit is provided at the request of a Utility company, the utility is required to reimburse the Department for the cost.

b. Mobilization. Use 5% of the total project cost for mobilization. Mobilization costs consist of preparatory work and operations necessary for the movement of personnel, equipment, supplies, and incidentals to and off the project site; for the establishment and removal of offices, buildings, and other facilities necessary for work on the project; and for all other work or operations that must be performed or costs incurred when beginning or ending work on the project.

c. Traffic Control. Maintaining traffic is a lump-sum item and the estimated cost is provided by the Traffic Engineering Division. Elements that should be considered include traffic volumes, traffic composition, peak times, number of lanes, length of construction, and type of work.

d. Existing Bridge Removal/Disposal. The cost of removing and disposing of an existing bridge is based on the project location, bridge type, bridge length and width, traffic control, type of crossing, historical data, and engineering judgment.

4. Engineering and Contingencies. Use between 10% and 15% of the total project cost for engineering and contingencies.

CONSTRUCTION COSTS: SOURCES AND IMPACTS

The Edison Foundation is a nonprofit organization dedicated to bringing the benefits of electricity to families, businesses, and industries worldwide.

Furthering Thomas Alva Edison's spirit of invention, the Foundation works to encourage a greater understanding of the production, delivery, and use of electric power to foster economic progress; to ensure a safe and clean environment; and to improve the quality of life for all people. The Edison Foundation provides knowledge, insight, and leadership to achieve its goals through research, conferences, grants, and other outreach activities.

The Brattle Group

The Brattle Group provides consulting services and expert testimony in economics, finance, and regulation to corporations, law firms, and public agencies worldwide. Our principals are internationally recognized experts, and we have strong partnerships with leading academics and highly credentialed industry specialists around the world.

INTRODUCTION AND EXECUTIVE SUMMARY

In *Why Are Electricity Prices Increasing? An Industry-Wide Perspective* (June 2006), *The Brattle Group* identified fuel and purchased-power cost increases as the primary driver of the electricity rate increases that consumers currently are facing. That report also noted that utilities are once again entering an infrastructure expansion phase, with significant investments in new baseload generating capacity, expansion of the bulk transmission system, distribution system enhancements, and new environmental controls. The report concluded that the industry could make the needed investments cost-effectively under a generally supportive rate environment.

The rate increase pressures arising from elevated fuel and purchased power prices continue. However, another major cost driver that was not explored in the previous work also will impact electric rates, namely, the substantial increases in the costs of building utility infrastructure projects.

Some of the factors underlying these construction cost trends are straightforward—such as sharp increases in materials cost—while others are complex, and sometimes less transparent in their impact.

Moreover, the recent rise in many utility construction cost components follows roughly a decade of relatively stable (or even declining) real construction costs, adding to the "sticker shock" that utilities experience when obtaining cost estimates or bids and that state public utility commissions experience during the process of reviewing applications for approvals to proceed with construction. While the full rate impact associated with construction cost increases will not be seen by customers until infrastructure projects are completed, the issue of rising construction costs currently affects industry investment plans and presents new challenges to regulators.

The purpose of this study is to a) document recent increases in the construction cost of utility infrastructure (generation, transmission, and distribution), b) identify the underlying causes of these increases, and c) explain how these increased costs will translate into higher rates that consumers might face as a result of required infrastructure investment. This report also provides a reference for utilities, regulators and the public to understand the issues related to recent construction cost increases. In summary, we find the following:

Dramatically increased raw materials prices (*e.g.*, steel, cement) have increased construction cost directly and indirectly through the higher cost of manufactured components common in utility infrastructure projects. These cost increases have primarily been due to high global demand for commodities and manufactured goods, higher production and transportation costs (in part owing to high fuel prices), and a weakening U.S. dollar.

Increased labor costs are a smaller contributor to increased utility construction costs, although that contribution may rise in the future as large construction projects across the country raise the demand for specialized and skilled labor over current or projected supply.

There also is a growing backlog of project contracts at large engineering, procurement and construction (EPC) firms, and construction management bids have begun to rise as a result. Although it is not possible to quantify the impact on future project bids by EPC firms, it is reasonable to assume that bids will become less cost-competitive as new construction projects are added to the queue. The price increases experienced over the past several years have affected all electric sector investment costs. In the generation sector, all technologies have experienced substantial cost increases in the past three years, from coal plants to windpower projects. Large proposed transmission projects have undergone cost revisions, and distribution system equipment costs have been rising rapidly.

Infrastructure costs were relatively stable during the 1990s, but have experienced substantial price increases in the past several years. Between January 2004 and January 2007, the costs of steam-generation plant, transmission projects and distribution equipment rose by 25 percent to 35 percent (compared to an 8 percent increase in the GDP deflator). For example, the cost of gas turbines, which was fairly steady in the early part of the decade, increased by 17 percent during the year 2006 alone.

As a result of these cost increases, the levelized capital cost component of baseload coal and nuclear plants has risen by \$20/MWh or more—substantially narrowing coal's overall cost advantages over natural gas-fired combined-cycle plants—and thus limiting some of the cost-reduction benefits expected from expanding the solid-fuel fleet.

The rapid increases experienced in utility construction costs have raised the price of recently completed infrastructure projects, but the impact has been mitigated somewhat to the extent that construction or materials acquisition preceded the most recent price increases.

The impact of rising costs has a more dramatic impact on the estimated cost of proposed utility infrastructure projects, which fully incorporates recent price trends. This has raised significant concerns that the next wave of utility investments may be imperiled by the high cost environment. These rising construction costs have also motivated utilities and regulators to more actively pursue energy efficiency and demand response initiatives in order to reduce the future rate impacts on consumers.

Despite the overwhelming evidence that construction costs have risen and will be elevated for some time, these increased costs are largely absent from the capital costs specified in the Energy Information Administration's (EIA's) 2007 *Annual Energy Outlook* (AEO). Since 2004, capital costs of all technologies are assumed to grow at the general price level—a pattern that contradicts the market evidence presented in this report. The growing divergence between the AEO data assumptions and recent cost escalation is now so substantial that the AEO data need to be adjusted to reflect recent cost increases to provide reliable indicators of current or future capital costs.

PROJECTED INVESTMENT NEEDS AND RECENT INFRASTRUCTURE COST INCREASES

Current and Projected U.S. Investment in Electricity Infrastructure The electric power industry is a very capital-intensive industry. The total value of generation, transmission and distribution infrastructure for regulated electric utilities is roughly $440 billion (property in service, net of accumulated depreciation and amortization), and capital expenditures are expected to exceed $70 billion in 2007.

Although the industry as a whole is always investing in capital, the rate of capital expenditures was relatively stable during the 1990s and began to rise near the turn of the century. As shown in *Why Are Electricity Prices Increasing? An Industry-Wide Perspective* (June 2006), utilities anticipate substantial increases in generation, transmission and distribution investment levels over the next two decades. Moreover, the significant need for new electricity infrastructure is a world-wide phenomenon: According to the *World Energy Investment Outlook 2006*, investments by power-sector companies throughout the world will total about $11 trillion dollars by 2030.

GENERATION

As of December 31, 2005, there were 988 gigawatts (GW) of electric generating capacity in service in the U.S., with the majority of this capacity owned by electric utilities. Close to 400 GW of this total, or 39 percent, consists of natural gas-fired capacity, with coal-based capacity comprising 32 percent, or slightly more than 300 GW, of the U.S. electric generation fleet.

Nuclear and hydroelectric plants comprise approximately 10 percent of the electric generation fleet. Approximately 49 percent of energy production is provided by coal plants, with 19 percent provided by nuclear plants. Natural gas-fired plants, which tend to operate as intermediate or peaking plants, also provided about 19 percent of U.S. energy production in 2006.

The need for installed generating capacity is highly correlated with load growth and projected growth in peak demand. According to EIA's most recent projections, U.S. electricity sales are expected to grow at an annual rate of about 1.4 percent through 2030.

According to the North American Electric Reliability Corporation (NERC), U.S. non-coincident peak demand is expected to grow by 19 percent (141 GW) from 2006 to 2015. According to EIA, utilities will need to build 258 GW of new generating capacity by 2030 to meet the projected growth in electricity demand and to replace old, inefficient plants that will be retired. EIA further projects that coal-based capacity, that is more capital intensive than natural gas-fired capacity which dominated new capacity additions over the last 15 years, will account for about 54 percent of total capacity additions from 2006 to 2030.

Natural gas-fired plants comprise 36 percent of the projected capacity additions in *AEO 2007*. EIA projects that the remaining 10 percent of capacity additions will be provided by renewable generators (6 percent) and nuclear power plants (4 percent). Renewable generators and nuclear power plants, similar to coal-based plants, are capital-intensive technologies with relatively high construction costs but low operating costs.

High-Voltage Transmission

The U.S. and Canadian electric transmission grid includes more than 200,000 miles of high voltage (230 kV and higher) transmission lines that ultimately serve more than 300 million customers.

This system was built over the past 100 years, primarily by vertically integrated utilities that generated and transmitted electricity locally for the benefit of their native load customers. Today, 134 control areas or balancing authorities manage electricity operations for local areas and coordinate reliability through the eight regional reliability councils of NERC.

After a long period of decline, transmission investment began a significant upward trend starting in the year 2000. Since the beginning of 2000, the industry has invested more than $37.8 billion in the nation's transmission system.

In 2006 alone, investor-owned electric utilities and stand-alone transmission companies invested an historic $6.9 billion in the nation's grid, while the Edison Electric Institute (EEI) estimates that utility transmission investments will increase to $8.0 billion during 2007. A recent EEI survey shows that its members plan to invest $31.5 billion in the transmission system from 2006 to 2009, a nearly 60-percent increase over the amount invested from 2002 to 2005.

These increased investments in transmission are prompted in part by the larger scale of base load generation additions that will occur farther from load centers, creating a need for larger and more costly transmission projects than those built over the past 20 years. In addition, new government policies and industry structures will contribute to greater transmission investment. In many parts of the country, transmission planning has been formally regionalized, and power markets create greater price transparency that highlights the value of transmission expansion in some instances.

NERC projects that 12,873 miles of new transmission will be added by 2015, an increase of 6.1 percent in the total miles of installed extra high-voltage (EHV) transmission lines (230 kV and above) in North America over the 2006 to 2015 period. NERC notes that this expansion lags demand growth and expansion of generating resources in most areas. However, NERC's figures do not include several major new transmission projects proposed in the PJM Interconnection LLC, such as the major new lines proposed by American Electric Power, Allegheny Power, and Pepco.

Distribution

While transmission systems move bulk power across wide areas, distribution systems deliver lower-voltage power to retail customers. The distribution system includes poles, as well as metering, billing, and other related infrastructure and software associated with retail sales and customer care functions. Continual investment in distribution facilities is needed, first and foremost, to keep pace with growth in customer demand. In real terms, investment began to increase in the mid-1990s, preceding the corresponding boom in generation.

This steady climb in investment in distribution assets shows no sign of diminishing. The need to replace an aging infrastructure, coupled with increased population growth and demand for power quality and customer service, is continuing to motivate utilities to improve their ultimate delivery system to customers. Continued customer load growth will require continued expansion in distribution system capacity. In 2006, utilities invested about

$17.3 billion in upgrading and expanding distribution systems, a 32-percent increase over the investment levels incurred in 2004. EEI projects that distribution investment during 2007 will again exceed $17.0 billion. While much of the recent increase in distribution investment reflects expanding physical infrastructure, a substantial portion of the increased dollar investment reflects the increased input costs of materials and labor to meet current distribution infrastructure needs.

Construction Costs for Recently Completed Generation

The majority of recently constructed plants have been either natural gas-fired or wind power plants. Both have displayed increasing real costs for several years. Since the 1990s, most of the new generating capacity built in the U.S. has been natural gas-fired capacity, either natural gas-fired combined-cycle units or natural gas-fired combustion turbines.

Combustion turbine prices recently rose sharply after years of real price decreases, while significant increases in the cost of installed natural gas combined-cycle combustion capacity have emerged during the past several years.

Using commercially available databases and other sources, such as financial reports, press releases and government documents, *The Brattle Group* collected data on the installation cost of natural gas-fired combined-cycle generating plants built in the U.S. during the last major construction cycle, defined as generating plants brought into service between 2000 and 2006.

We estimated that the average real construction cost of all natural gas-fired combined-cycle units brought online between 2000 and 2006 was approximately $550/kilowatt (kW) (in 2006 dollars), with a range of costs between $400/

kW to approximately $1,000/kW. Statistical analysis confirmed that real installation cost was influenced by plant size, the turbine technology, the NERC region in which the plant was located, and the commercial online date.

Notably, we found a positive and statistically significant relationship between a plant's construction cost and its online date, meaning that, everything else equal, the later a plant was brought online, the higher its real installation cost.

Another major class of generation development during this decade has been wind generation, the costs of which have also increased in recent years. The Northwest Power and Conservation Council (NPCC), a regional planning council that prepares long-term electric resource plans for the Pacific Northwest, issued its most recent review of the cost of wind power in July 2006.

The Council found that the cost of new wind projects rose substantially in real terms in the last two years, and was much higher than that assumed in its most recent resource plan.

Specifically, the Council found that the levelized lifecycle cost of power for new wind projects rose 50 to 70 percent, with higher construction costs being the principal contributor to this increased cost. According to the Council, the construction cost of wind projects, in real dollars, has increased from about $1150/kW to $1300-$1700/kW in the past few years, with an unweighted average capital cost of wind projects in 2006 at $1,485/kW.

Factors contributing to the increase in wind power costs include a weakening dollar, escalation of commodity and energy costs, and increased demand for wind power under renewable portfolio standards established by a growing number of states. The Council notes that commodities used in the manufacture and installation of wind turbines and ancillary equipment, including cement, copper, steel and resin have experienced significant cost increases in recent years. These observations were confirmed recently in a May 2007 report by the U.S. Department of Energy (DOE), which found that prices for wind turbines (the primary cost component of installed wind capacity) rose by more than $400/kW between 2002 and 2006, a nearly 60-percent increase.

Wind Turbine Prices 1997 -2007

Rising Projected Construction Costs: Examples and Case Studies

Although recently completed gas-fired and wind-powered capacity has shown steady real cost increases in recent years, the most dramatic cost escalation figures arise from *proposed* utility investments, which fully reflect the recent, sharply rising prices of various components of construction and installation costs.

The most visible of these are generation proposals, although several transmission proposals also have undergone substantial upward cost revisions. Distribution-level investments are smaller and less discrete ("lumpy") and thus are not subject to similar ongoing public scrutiny on a project-by-project basis.

Coal-Based Power Plants

Evidence of the significant increase in the construction cost of coal-based power plants can be found in recent applications filed by utilities, such as Duke Energy and Otter Tail Power Company, seeking regulatory approval to build such plants. Otter Tail Power Company leads a consortium of seven Midwestern utilities that are seeking to build a 630-MW coal-based generating unit (Big Stone II) on the site of the existing Big Stone Plant near Milbank, South Dakota. In addition, the developers of Big Stone II seek to build a new high-voltage transmission line to deliver power from Big Stone II and from other sources, including possibly wind and other renewable forms of energy. Initial cost estimates for the power plant were about $1 billion, with an additional $200 million for the transmission line project. However, these cost estimates increased dramatically, largely due to higher costs for construction materials and labor.

Based on the most recent design refinements, the project, including transmission, is expected to cost $1.6 billion. In June 2006, Duke submitted a filing with the North Carolina Utilities Commission (NCUC) seeking a certificate of public convenience and necessity for the construction of two 800 MW coal-based generating units at the site of the existing Cliffside Steam Station. In its initial application, Duke relied on a May 2005 preliminary cost estimate showing that the two units would cost approximately $2 billion to build.

Five months later, Duke submitted a second filing with a significantly revised cost estimate. In its second filing, Duke estimated that the two units would cost approximately $3 billion to build, a 50 percent cost increase.

The North Carolina Utilities Commission approved the construction of one 800 MW unit at Cliffside but disapproved the other unit, primarily on the basis that Duke had not made a showing that it needed the capacity to serve projected native load demands.

Duke's latest projected cost for building one 800 MW unit at Cliffside is approximately $1.8 billion, or about $2,250/kW. When financing costs, or allowance for funds used during construction (AFUDC), are included, the total cost is estimated to be $2.4 billion (or about $3,000/kW).

Rising construction costs have also led utilities to reconsider expansion plans prior to regulatory actions. In

December 2006, Westar Energy announced that it was deferring the consideration of a new 600 MW coal-based generation facility due to significant increases in the estimated construction costs, which increased from $1.0 billion to about $1.4 billion since the plant was first announced in May 2005.

Increased construction costs are also affecting proposed demonstration projects. For example, DOE announced earlier this year that the projected cost for one of its most prominent clean coal demonstration project, FutureGen, had nearly doubled.

FutureGen is a clean coal demonstration project being pursued by a public-private partnership involving DOE and an alliance of industrial coal producers and electric utilities. FutureGen is an experimental advanced Integrated Gasification Combined Cycle (IGCC) coal plant project that will aim for near zero emissions of sulfur dioxide (SO_2), nitrogen oxides (NOx), mercury, particulates and carbon dioxide (CO_2).

Its initial cost was estimated at $950 million. But after re-evaluating the price of construction materials and labor and adjusting for inflation over time, DOE's Office of Fossil Energy announced that the project's price had increased to $1.7 billion.

Transmission Projects

NSTAR, the electric distribution company that serves the Boston metropolitan area, recently built two 345 kV lines from a switching station in Stoughton, Massachusetts, to substations in the Hyde Park section of Boston and to South Boston, respectively.

In an August 2004 filing before ISO New England Inc. (ISO-NE), NSTAR indicated that the project would cost $234.2 million. In March 2007, NSTAR informed ISO-NE that estimated project costs had increased by $57.7 million, or almost 25 percent, for a revised total project cost of $292 million. NSTAR stated that the increase is driven by increases in both construction and material costs, with construction bids coming in 24 percent higher than initially estimated.

NSTAR further explained that there have been dramatic increases in material costs, with copper costs increasing by 160 percent, core steel by 70 percent, flow-fill concrete by 45 percent, and dielectric fluid (used for cable cooling) by 66 percent.

Another aspect of transmission projects is land requirements, and in many areas of the country land prices have increased substantially in the past few years. In March 2007, the California Public Utilities Commission (CPUC) approved construction of the Southern California Edison (SCE) Company's proposed 25.6-mile, 500 kV transmission line between SCE's existing Antelope and Pardee Substations.

SCE initially estimated a cost of $80.3 million for the Antelope-Pardee 500 kV line. However, the company subsequently revised its estimate by updating the anticipated cost of acquiring a right-of-way, reflecting a rise in California's real estate prices. The increased land acquisition costs increased the total estimate for the project to $92.5 million, increasing the estimated costs to more than $3.5 million per mile.

Distribution Equipment

Although most individual distribution projects are small relative to the more visible and public generation and transmission projects, costs have been rising in this sector as well. This is most readily seen in Handy-Whitman Index price series relating to distribution equipment and components. Several important categories of distribution equipment have experienced sharp price increases over the past three years. For example, the prices of line transformers and pad transformers have increased by 68 percent and 79 percent, respectively, between January 2004 and January 2007, with increases during 2006 alone of 28 percent and 23 percent.

The cost of overhead conductors and devices increased over the past three years by 34 percent, and the cost of station equipment rose by 38 percent. These are in contrast to the overall price increases (measured by the GDP deflator) of roughly 8 percent over the past three years.

FACTORS SPURRING RISING CONSTRUCTION COSTS

Broadly speaking, there are four primary sources of the increase in construction costs:

(1) material input costs, including the cost of raw physical inputs, such as steel and cement as well as increased costs of components manufactured from these inputs (*e.g.*, transformers, turbines, pumps);

(2) shop and fabrication capacity for manufactured components (relative to current demand);

(3) the cost of construction field labor, both unskilled and craft labor; and

(4) the market for large construction project management, *i.e.*, the queuing and bidding for projects. This section will discuss each of these factors.

Material Input Costs

Utility construction projects involve large quantities of steel, aluminum and copper (and components manufactured from these metals) as well as cement for foundations, footings and structures. All of these commodities have experienced substantial recent price increases, due to increased domestic and global demands as well as increased energy costs in mineral extraction, processing and transportation. In addition, since many of these materials are traded globally, the recent performance of the U.S. dollar will impact the domestic costs.

Metals

After being relatively stable for many years (and even declining in real terms), the price of various metals, including steel, copper and aluminum, has increased significantly in the last few years.

These increases are primarily the result of high global demand and increased production costs (including the impact of high energy prices). A weakening U.S. dollar has also contributed to high domestic prices for imported metals and various component products.

The price of both inputs fell in real terms during the late 1990s, but rose sharply after 2002. Compared to the 20-percent increase in the general inflation rate (GDP deflator) between 1997 and 2006, iron ore prices rose 75 percent and iron and steel scrap prices rose nearly 120 percent. The increase over the last few years was especially sharp—between 2003 and 2006, prices for iron ore rose 60 percent and iron and scrap steel rose 150 percent.

Exchange Rates

Many of the raw materials involved in utility construction projects (e.g., steel, copper, cement), as well as many major manufactured components of utility infrastructure investments, are globally traded. This means that prices in the U.S. are also affected by exchange rate fluctuations, which have been adverse to the dollar in recent years. The chart below shows trade-weighted exchange rates from 1997. Although the dollar appreciated against other currencies between 1997 and 2001, the graph also clearly shows a substantial erosion of the dollar since the beginning of 2002, losing roughly 20 percent of its value against other major trading partners' currencies. This has had a substantial impact on U.S. material and manufactured component prices, as will be reflected in many of the graphs that follow.

The increase in input prices has been reflected in steel mill product prices. Figure 6 compares the trend in steel mill product prices to the general inflation rate (using the GDP deflator) over the past 10 years. Various sources point to the rapid growth of steel production and demand in China as a primary cause of the increases in both steel prices and the prices of steelmaking inputs.China has become both the world's largest steelmaker and steel consumer.

In addition, some analysts contend that steel companies have achieved greater pricing power, partly due to ongoing consolidation of the industry, and note that recently increased demand for steel has been driven largely by products used in energy and heavy industry, such as plate and structural steels.

From the perspective of the steel industry, the substantial and at least semi-permanent rise in the price of steel has been justified by the rapid rise in the price of many steelmaking inputs, such as steel scrap, iron ore, coking coal, and natural gas. Today's steel prices remain at historically elevated levels and, based on the underlying causes for high prices described, it appears that iron and steel costs are likely to remain at these high levels at least for the near future.

Other metals important for utility infrastructure display similar price patterns: declining real prices over the first five years or so of the previous 10 years, followed by sharp increases in the last few years. These price increases were also evident in metals that contribute to important steel alloys used broadly in electrical infrastructure, such as nickel and tungsten. The prices of these display similar patterns.

Cement, Concrete, Stone and Gravel

Large infrastructure projects require huge amounts of cement as well as basic stone materials. The price of cement has also risen substantially in the past few years, for the same reasons cited above for metals.

Cement is an energy-intensive commodity that is traded on international markets, and recent price patterns resemble those displayed for metals. In utility construction, cement is often combined with stone and other aggregates for concrete (often reinforced with steel), and there are other site uses for sand, gravel and stone. These materials have also undergone significant price increases, primarily as a result of increased energy costs in extraction and transportation. Prices for these materials have increased about 30 percent between 2004 and 2006.

Manufactured Products for Utility Infrastructure

Although large utility construction projects consume substantial amounts of unassembled or semi-finished metal products (*e.g.*, reinforcing bars for concrete, structural steel), many of the components such as conductors, transformers and other equipment are manufactured elsewhere and shipped to the construction site. Available price indices for these components display similar patterns of recent sharp price increases.

Manufactured components of generating facilities—large pressure vessels, condensers, pumps, valves—have also increased sharply since 2004.

Labor Costs

A significant component of utility construction costs is labor—both unskilled (common) labor as well as craft labor such as pipefitters and electricians. Labor costs have also increased at rates higher than the general inflation rate, although more steadily since 1997, and recent increases have been less dramatic than for commodities. A composite national labor cost index based on simple averages of the regional Handy-Whitman Index for common and craft labor. Between January 2001 and January 2007, the general inflation rate (measured by the GDP deflator) increased about 15 percent.

During the same period, the cost of craft labor and heavy construction labor increased about 26 percent, while common labor increased 27 percent, or almost twice the rate of general inflation. While less severe than commodity cost increases, increased labor costs contributed to the overall construction cost increases because of their substantial share in overall utility infrastructure construction costs.

Although labor costs have not risen dramatically in recent years, there is growing concern about an emerging gap between demand and supply of skilled construction labor—especially if the anticipated boom in utility construction materializes. In 2002, the Construction Users Roundtable (CURT), surveyed its members and found that recruitment, education, and retention of craft workers continue to be critical issues for the industry.

The average age of the current construction skilled workforce is rising rapidly, and high attrition rates in construction are compounding the problem. The industry has always had high attrition at the entry-level positions, but now many workers in the 35-40 year-old age group are leaving the industry for a variety of reasons. The latest projections indicate that, because of attrition and anticipated growth, the construction industry must recruit 200,000 to 250,000 new craft workers per year to meet future needs. However, both demographics and a poor industry image are working against the construction industry as it tries to address this need.

There also could be a growing gap between the demand and supply of electrical lineworkers who maintain the electric grid and who perform much of the labor for transmission and distribution investments. These workers erect poles and transmission towers and install or repair cables or wires used to carry electricity from power plants to customers. According to a DOE report, demand for such workers is expected to outpace supply over the next decade.

The DOE analysis indicates a significant forecasted shortage in the availability of qualified candidates by as many as 10,000 lineworkers, or nearly 20 percent of the current workforce. As of 2005, lineworkers earned a mean hourly wage of $25/hour, or $52,300 per year. The forecast supply shortage will place upward pressure on the wages earned by lineworkers.

Shop and Fabrication Capacity

Many of the components of utility projects—including large components like turbines, condensers, and transformers—are manufactured, often as special orders to coincide with particular construction projects.

Because many of these components are not held in large inventories, the overall capacity of their manufacturers can influence the prices obtained and the length of time between order and delivery. While equipment and component prices obviously reflect underlying material costs, some of the price increases of manufactured components and the delivery lags are due to manufacturing capacity constraints that are not readily overcome in the near term.

Recent orders have largely eliminated spare shop capacity, and delivery times for major manufactured components have risen. These constraints are adding to price increases and are difficult to overcome with imported components because of the lower value of the dollar in recent years.

The increased delivery times can affect utility construction costs through completion delays that increase the cost of financing a project. In general, utilities commit substantial funds during the construction phase of a project that have to be financed either through debt or equity, called "allowance for fund used during construction" (AFUDC). All else held equal, the longer the time from the initiation through completion of a project, the higher is the financing costs of the investment and the ultimate costs passed through to ratepayers.

ENGINEERING, PROCUREMENT AND CONSTRUCTION (EPC) MARKET CONDITIONS

Increased worldwide demand for new generating and other electric infrastructure projects, particularly in China, has been cited as a significant reason for the recent escalation in the construction cost of new power plants. This suggests that major Engineering, Procurement and Construction (EPC) firms should have a growing backlog of utility infrastructure projects in the pipeline.

While we were unable to obtain specific information from the major EPC firms on their worldwide backlog of electric utility infrastructure projects (*i.e.*, the number of electric utility projects compared with other infrastructure projects such as roads, port facilities and water infrastructure, in their respective pipelines), we examined their financial statements, which specify the financial value associated with their backlog of infrastructure projects. This significant increase in the annual backlog of infrastructure projects at EPC firms is consistent with the data showing an increased worldwide demand for infrastructure projects in general and also utility generation, transmission, and distribution projects.

The growth in construction project backlogs likely will dampen the competitiveness of EPC bids for future projects, at least until the EPC industry is able to expand capacity to manage and execute greater volumes of projects. This observation does not imply that this market is generally uncompetitive—rather it reflects the limited ability of EPC firms with near-term capacity constraints to service an upswing in new project development associated with a boom period in infrastructure construction cycles. Such constraints, combined with a rapidly filling (or full) queue for project management services, limit incentives to bid aggressively on new projects.

Although difficult to quantify, this lack of spare capacity in the EPC market will undoubtedly have an upward price pressure on new bids for EPC services and contracts. A recent filing by Oklahoma Gas & Electric Company (OG&E) seeking approval of the Red Rock plant (a 950 MW coal unit) provides a demonstration of this effect. In January 2007, OG&E testimony indicated that their February 3, 2006, cost estimate of nearly $1,700/kW had been revised to more than $1,900/kW by September 29, 2006, a 12-percent increase in just nine months. More than half of the increase (6.6 percent) was ascribed to change in market conditions which "reflect higher materials costs (steel and concrete), escalation in major equipment costs, and a significant tightening of the market for EPC contractor services (as there are relatively few qualified firms that serve the power plant development market)."

In the detailed cost table, OG&E indicated that the estimate for EPC services had increased by more than 50 percent during the nine month period (from \$223/kW to \$340/kW).

Summary Construction Cost Indices

Several sources publish summary construction cost indices that reflect composite costs for various construction projects. Although changes in these indices depend on the actual cost weights assumed *e.g.*, labor, materials, manufactured components, they provide useful summary measures for large infrastructure project construction costs.

The RSMeans Construction Cost Index provides a general construction cost index, which reflects primarily building construction (as opposed to utility projects).

This index also reflects many of the same cost drivers as large utility construction projects such as steel, cement and labor. The changes in the RSMeans Construction Cost index since 1990 relative to the general inflation rate. While the index rose slightly higher than the GDP deflator beginning in the mid 1990s, it shows a pronounced increase between 2003 and 2006 when it rose by 18 percent compared to the 9 percent increase in general inflation.

The index numbers displayed on the graphs are for January 1 of each year displayed. Between January 1, 2004, and January 1, 2007, the cost of constructing steam generating units increased by 25 percent—more than triple the rate of inflation over the same time period.

The cost of gas turbogenerators (combustion turbines), on the other hand, actually fell between 2003 and 2005. However, during 2006, the cost of a new combustion turbine increased by nearly 18 percent—roughly 10 times the rate of general inflation. The increased cost of transmission investment, which reflects such items as towers, poles, station equipment, conductors and conduit. The cost of transmission plant investments rose at about the rate of inflation between 1991 and 2000, increased in 2001, and then showed an especially sharp increase between 2004 and 2007, rising almost 30 percent or nearly four times the annual inflation rate over that period.

Overall distribution plant costs tracked the general inflation rate very closely between 1991 and 2003. However, it then increased 34 percent between January 2004 and January 2007, a rate that exceeded four times the rate of general inflation.

COMPARISON WITH ENERGY INFORMATION ADMINISTRATION POWER PLANT COST ESTIMATES

Every year, EIA prepares a long-term forecast of energy prices, production, and consumption (for electricity and the other major energy sectors), which is documented in the *Annual Energy Outlook* (AEO).

A companion publication, *Assumptions to the Annual Energy Outlook*, itemizes the assumptions (*e.g.*, fuel prices, economic growth, environmental regulation) underlying EIA's annual long-term forecast. Included in the latter document are estimates of the "overnight" capital cost of new generating units *(i.e.,* the capital cost exclusive of financing costs). These cost estimates influence the type of new generating capacity projected to be built during the 25-year time horizon modeled in the AEO.

The EIA capital cost assumptions are generic estimates that do not take into account the site-specific characteristics that can affect construction costs significantly.

While EIA's estimates do not necessarily provide an accurate estimate of the cost of building a power plant at a specific location, they should, in theory, provide a good "ballpark" estimate of the relative construction cost of different generation technologies at any given time. In addition, since they are prepared annually, these estimates also should provide insight into construction cost trends over time.

The EIA plant cost estimates are widely used by industry analysts, consultants, academics, and policymakers. These numbers frequently are cited in regulatory proceedings, sometimes as a yardstick by which to measure a utility's projected or incurred capital costs for a generating plant. Given this, it is important that EIA's numbers provide a reasonable estimate of plant costs and incorporate both technological and other market trends that significantly affect these costs.

We reviewed EIA's estimate of overnight plant costs for the six-year period 2001 to 2006. EIA's estimates of the construction cost of six generation technologies—combined-cycle gas-fired plants, combustion turbines (CTs), pulverized coal, nuclear, IGCC, and wind—over the period 2001 to 2006 and compares these projections to the general inflation rate (GDP deflator).

These six technologies, generally speaking, have been the ones most commonly built or given serious consideration in utility resource plans over the last few years. Thus, we can compare the data and case studies discussed above to EIA's cost estimates.

The two exceptions to this are conventional coal and IGCC, which increase by a near constant rate each year close to the rate of inflation throughout the period.

The data show conventional CC and conventional CT experiencing a sharp increase between 2001 and 2002. After this increase, conventional CC levels off and proceeds to increase at a pace near inflation, while conventional CT actually drops significantly before 2004 when it too levels near the rate of inflation. The pattern seen with nuclear technology is near to the opposite. It falls dramatically until about 2003 and then increases at the same rate as the GDP deflator. Lastly, wind moves close to inflation until 2004 when it experiences a one-time jump and then flattens off through 2006.

These patterns of cost estimates over time contradict the data and findings of this report. Almost every other generation construction cost element has shown price changes at or near the rate of inflation throughout the early part of this decade with a dramatic change in only the last few years.

EIA appears to have reconsidered several technology cost estimates (or revised the benchmark technology type) in isolation between 2001 and 2004, without a systematic update of others. Meanwhile, during the period that overall construction costs were rising well above the general inflation rate, EIA has not revised its estimated capital cost figures to reflect this trend.

EIA's estimates of plant costs do not adequately reflect the recent increase in plant construction costs that has occurred in the last few years. Indeed, EIA itself acknowledges that its estimated construction costs do not reflect short-term changes in the price of commodities such as steel, cement and concrete.

While one would expect some lag in the EIA data, it is troubling that its most recent estimates continue to show the construction cost of conventional power plants increasing only at the general rate of inflation.

Empirical evidence shows that the construction cost of generating plants—both fossil-fired and renewable—is escalating at a rate well above the GDP deflator. Even the most recent EIA data fail to reflect important market impacts that are driving plant construction costs, and thus do not provide a reliable measure of current or expected construction costs.

CONCLUSION

Construction costs for electric utility investments have risen sharply over the past several years, due to factors beyond the industry's control. Increased prices for material and manufactured components, rising wages, and a tighter market for construction project management services have contributed to an across-the-board increase in the costs of investing in utility infrastructure. These higher costs show no immediate signs of abating.

Despite these higher costs, utilities will continue to invest in baseload generation, environmental controls, transmission projects and distribution system expansion. However, rising construction costs will put additional upward pressure on retail rates over time, and may alter the pace and composition of investments going forward. The overall impact on the industry and on customers, however, will be borne out in various ways, depending on how utilities, markets and regulators respond to these cost increases. In the long run, customers ultimately will pay for higher construction costs—either directly in rates for completed assets of regulated companies, less directly in the form of higher energy prices needed to attract new generating capacity in organized markets and in higher transmission tariffs, or indirectly when rising construction costs defer investments and delay expected benefits such as enhanced reliability and lower, more stable long-term electricity prices.

3

Measuring the Costs of Production

Costs are defined as those expenses faced by a business in the process of supplying goods and services to consumers. In the short run (where there are fixed and variable factors of production) we make a distinction between fixed and variable costs. Examples of each are given below.

Short Run Costs of Production

TOTAL COSTS (TC) = TOTAL FIXED COST (TFC) + TOTAL VARIABLE COSTS (TVC)

Fixed Costs

Fixed costs relate to the fixed factors of production and do not vary directly with the level of output. (I.e. they are exogenous of the level of production in the short run).

Good examples to use are rent of buildings, leasing of capital equipment, the annual uniform business rate charged by local authorities, the costs of full-time contracted salaried staff, interest rates on loans, the depreciation of fixed capital (due to age) and the costs of business insurance.

Total fixed costs (TFC) remain constant as output increases. Average fixed cost (AFC) = Total Fixed Costs (TFC) / Output (Q) Average fixed costs will fall continuously with output because the total fixed costs are being spread over a higher level of production causing the average cost to fall.

Examples of Fixed Costs

Rent of buildings, leasing of plant and equipment, local business rates, the costs of salaried staff, interest rates on loans, depreciation of capital (due to age) and insurance premiums.

Average fixed cost (AFC) = Total Fixed Costs (TFC)

Output (Q)

An increase in fixed costs has no effect at all on the variable costs of production. This means that only the average total cost curve shifts. There is no change at all on the marginal cost curve leading to no change in the profit maximising price and output of a business.

Average fixed costs will fall continuously with output because the total fixed costs are being spread over a higher level of production causing the average cost to fall

Average fixed costs falls as output increases. A business can "spread their over head costs" by increasing output in the short run. Average fixed cost will never be zero if there are positive total fixed costs.

Variable Costs

These are costs that vary directly with output since more variable units are required to increase output. Examples are the costs of essential raw materials and components, the wages of part-time staff or employees paid by the hour, the costs of electricity and gas and depreciation of capital inputs due to wear and tear. Total variable cost rises as output increases.

Average variable cost (AVC) = Total Variable Costs (TVC) /Output (Q) AVC depends on the cost of employing variable factors compared to the average productivity of these factors (usually labour productivity). If additional units of labour can be hired at a constant cost there will be an inverse relationship between average product and average variable cost. Therefore, when average product is maximised, AVC will be minimised.

COST-OF-PRODUCTION THEORY OF VALUE

In economics, the cost-of-production theory of value is the theory that the price of an object is determined by the sum of the cost of the resources that went into making it. The cost can compose any of the factors of production (including labour, capital, or land) and taxation.

The theory makes the most sense under assumptions of constant returns to scale and the existence of just one non-produced factor of production. These are the assumptions of the so-called non-substitution theorem. Under these assumptions, the long run price of a commodity is equal to the sum of the cost of the inputs into that commodity, including interest charges.

Historically, the most well known proponent of such theories is probably Adam Smith. Piero Sraffa, in his introduction to the first volume of the "Collected Works of David Ricardo", referred to Adam Smith's adding up theory. Smith contrasted natural prices with market prices.

Smith theorized that market prices would tend towards natural prices, where outputs would be at what he characterized as the "level of effectual demand". At this level, Smith's natural prices of commodities are the sum of the natural rates of wages, profits, and rent that must be paid for inputs into production. (Smith is ambiguous about whether rent is price-determining or price determined The latter view is the consensus of later classical economists with the Ricardo-Malthus-West theory of rent.)

David Ricardo mixed such cost of production theory of prices with the labor theory of value, as that latter theory was understood by Eugen von Bohm-Bawerk and others. This is the theory that prices tend toward proportionality to the socially necessary labor embodied in a commodity. Ricardo sets this theory at the start of the first chapter of his "Principles of Political Economy and Taxation". Ricardo also refutes the labor theory of value in later sections of that chapter.

This refutation leads to what later became known as the transformation problem. Karl Marx later takes up that theory in the first volume of "Capital", while indicating that he is quite aware that the theory is untrue at lower levels of abstraction. This has led to all sorts of arguments over what both David Ricardo and Karl Marx "really meant". Nevertheless, it seems undeniable that all the major classical economics and Marx explicitly rejected the labor theory of price).

A somewhat different theory of cost-determined prices is provided by the "neo-Ricardian school" of Piero Sraffa and his followers.

The Polish economist Micha³ Kalecki distinguished between sectors with "cost-determined prices" (such as manufacturing and services) and those with "demand-determined prices" (such as agriculture and raw material extraction).

One might think of this theory as equivalent to modern theories of markup-pricing, full-cost pricing, or administrative pricing. Ever since Hall and Hitch, economists have found that the evidence gathered in surveys of businessmen support such theories.

Most contemporary economists accept neoclassical economics or mainstream economics. The non-substitution theorem is presented in graduate level microeconomics textbooks as a theorem of mainstream economics. Also many mainstream economists think they can justify theories of full-cost pricing within their theory. The majority of mainstream economists would probably then accept this theory as an element in their theory which does not give adequate attention to issues of consumer demand and marginal utility.

Market Price

Market price is an economic concept with commonplace familiarity; it is the price that a good or service is offered at, or will fetch, in the marketplace; it is of interest mainly in the study of microeconomics. Market value and market price are equal only under conditions of market efficiency, equilibrium, and rational expectations.

In economics, returns to scale and economies of scale are related terms that describe what happens as the scale of production increases. They are different terms and are not to be used interchangeably.

Marginal Utility

An individual will typically be able to partially order the potential uses of a good or service. For example, a ration of water might be used to sustain oneself, a dog, or a rose bush. Say that a given person gives her own sustenance highest priority, that of the dog next highest priority, and lowest priority to saving the roses. In that case, if the individual has two rations of water, then the marginal utility of either of those rations is that of sustaining the dog. The marginal utility of a third gallon would be that of watering the roses.

(The *diminishing* of utility should not necessarily be taken to be itself an arithmetic subtraction. It may be no more than a purely ordinal change.)

The notion that marginal utilities are diminishing across the ranges relevant to decision-making is called "the law of diminishing marginal utility" (and also known as a "Gossen's First Law").

However, it will not always hold. The case of the person, dog, and roses is one in which potential uses operate independently — there is no complementarity across the three uses. Sometimes an amount added brings things past a desired tipping point, or an amount subtracted causes them to fall short. In such cases, the marginal utility of a good or service might actually be increasing.

Labor Theory of Value

The labor theories of value (LTV) are theories in economics according to which the true values of commodities are related to the labor needed to produce them.

There are many different accounts of labor value, with the common element that the "value" of an exchangeable good or service is, or ought to be, or tends to be, or can be considered as, equal or proportional to the amount of labor required to produce it (including the labor required to produce the raw materials and machinery used in production).

Different labor theories of value prevailed amongst classical economists through to the mid-19th century. It is especially associated with Adam Smith and David Ricardo. Since that time it is most often associated with Marxian economics; while among modern mainstream economists it is considered to be superseded by the marginal utility approach.

PRODUCTION, COSTS, AND PRICING

In microeconomics, production is the act of making things, in particular the act of making products that will be traded or sold commercially. Production decisions concentrate on what goods to produce, how to produce them, the costs of producing them, and optimizing the mix of resource inputs used in their production. This production information can then be combined with market information (like demand and marginal revenue) to determine the quantity of products to produce and the optimum 'pricing'(Imaga, 1994: 384).

(In macroeconomics, production is measured by gross domestic product and other measures of national income and output.)

Aspects of Production and Pricing Theory

- Production theory basics
  * production efficiency
  * factors of production
  * total, average, and marginal product curves
  * marginal productivity
  * isoquants & isocosts
  * the marginal rate of technical substitution
- Economic rent
  * classical factor rents
  * Paretian factor rents
- Equilibrium income distribution
- Production possibility frontier
  * what products are possible given your resources
  * the trade-off between producing one product rather than another
  * the marginal rate of transformation
- Production function
  * inputs

  * diminishing returns to inputs
  * the stages of production
  * shifts in a production function
- Cost theory
  * the different types of costs
    — opportunity cost
    — accounting cost or historical costs
    — transaction cost
    — sunk cost
    — marginal cost
  * the isocost line
- Cost-of-production theory of value
- Long-run cost and production functions
  * long-run average cost
  * long-run production function and efficiency
  * returns to scale and isoclines
  * minimum efficient scale
  * plant capacity
- Economies of density
- Economies of scale
  * the efficiency consequences of increasing or decreasing the level of production
- Economies of scope
  * the efficiency consequences of increasing or decreasing the number of different types of products produced, promoted, and distributed
- Optimum factor allocation
  * output elasticity of factor costs
  * marginal revenue product

  * marginal resource cost
- Pricing
  * various aspects of the pricing decision
- Transfer pricing
  * selling within a multi-divisional company
- Joint product pricing
  * price setting when two products are linked
- Price discrimination
  * different prices to different buyers
  * types of price discrimination
  * yield management
- Price skimming
  * price discrimination over time
- Two part tariffs
  * charging a price comprised of two parts, usually an initial fee and an ongoing fee
- Price points
  * the effects of a non-linear demand curve on pricing
- Cost-plus pricing
  * a markup is applied to a cost term in order to calculate price
  * cost-plus pricing with elasticity considerations
  * cost plus pricing is often used along with break even analysis
- Rate of return pricing
  * calculate price based on the required rate of return on investment, or rate of return on sales
- Profit maximization
  * determining the optimum price and quantity

* the totals approach
* the marginal approach of production

Production Systems

Mass Production

Characteristics

- Equipment is expensive and used for a solitary purpose.
- A very small variety of goods are produced.
- Goods are transported from one fixed work station to another.

Advantages

- Greater specialisation.
- Optimum utilisation of workers and machinery.
- Low production costs per unit.
- Low stock-piling costs.
- Restricted handling of materials.
- Production control is simplified.
- High sales earning profit.
- Division of labour.
- Equipment standardized.
- Products uniform.

Disadvantages

- Expensive capital for equipments/machineries.

Jobbing

Characteristics

- General, all-purpose machinery.
- Products are generally capital goods.
- One task must be completed before the next may commence.

- Customers give specifications.
- Production processes are seldom repeated.
- Workers must be highly skilled.
- Control of production is simple.

Batch Production

Characteristics

- Falls between mass production and jobbing.
- One batch of products must be completed before work on the next one may begin.
- Customers give their specifications.
- Similar products produced on a batch basis, in large quantities.

Advantages

- Greater flexibility in terms of quantity produced, factory layout and manufacturing process.
- Can adjust to changes in demand.
- Less time wasted during machinery-breakdowns.
- Less expensive machinery.

Disadvantages

- Products take longer to produce.
- Larger quantities of semi-finished goods must be kept, hence increasing stockpiling costs.
- Cost per unit is generally higher.
- Careful planning needed to use this method effectively

FACTORY LAYOUT

Advantages of a Proper Factory Layout

For Workers

- Less exertion

- Less handling
- Happier and more productive in pleasant working conditions
- Fewer accidents

For Company

- Less working capital required
- Less money invested in stock
- Increase in factory safety
- Easier production control
- Lower labour, maintenance and transport costs
- High production yield
- Fewer labourer; fewer salaries and wages to pay

Requirements of a Good Factory Layout

- Practical and economical
- Complies with government safety regulations
- Adaptable
- Promote workers' health
- Maximum space (vertical and horizontal) utilised
- A logical, consecutive process
- Materials have to travel the shortest possible distance.

Factory Plant and Machinery

Types of Machinery

- Standard machines are built on a broad scale and are easier to maintain. They are used for batch production and jobbing.
- Specialised machines are built to specific requirements and are difficult to resell. They are used for mass production.

Factors to Consider when Purchasing Machinery

- Lifespan
- Training that workers might require
- Availability of replacements
- Effect on factory layout
- Cost of purchase and maintenance
- Resale value
- Utilisation period per day
- Whether or not it can be utilised economically
- Rate of production
- Accuracy
- Availability of parts
- Rate of Lun

Maintenance

- Remedial maintenance — complete overhaul when machinery breaks down
- Preventative maintenance — minor or major repair to prevent breakdown
- Conditional maintenance — inspection of condition

Product Specification and Methods of Production

Product specification refers to anything which describes how a product will be manufactured.

Product Planning and Control

Advantages of Efficient Planning

For the supplier of raw materials

- Assured of a continued relationship with the factory
- Assured of regular orders from the factory

For the dealer

- Regular supply at a reasonable price
- Assured against having to search for suppliers all the time
- Usually assured of a certain quality, quantity and timeous and correct delivery
- Costs reduced

For the worker

- Job satisfaction is promoted.
- Healthy and safe working environment
- May result in improved wages or salaries
- Knowledge of what is expected

For the consumer

- Regular supply at right place and time
- Lower prices due to reduced production costs

Quality control: This is a system for determining at which points in the production process deviations and deficiencies emerge.

How to go about setting quality control

- Workers and inspectors must be made well aware of the prerequisite standards, and tolerances must be set.
- A suitable number of inspection points must be decided upon.
- Reliable testing and inspecting measures must be used.
- A suitable number of inspections per inspection point must be decided upon.

Advantages of quality control

- Dealers and customers are assured of the quality of the goods that they are purchasing.

- It can serve as a reliable basis for wage incentive schemes.
- Workers are encourage to continue to produce goods of a certain standard.
- Production costs can be lowered.
- It can lead to improved product design and quality.

Work study (time and motion only)

- Work study is a scientific measure of working methods, with the aim of finding more effective methods, machinery and materials, standardising them and determining a standard time for every method.
- Method study analyses all working methods and the organisation of machinery with a mind to finding more effective production methods.
- Work measurement is an evaluation of exactly how long it takes suitably skilled workers, labouring at maximum tempo (without adversely affecting health) with standard and according to stipulated requirements, to complete a given task.

Safety measures

- Hygiene requirements for workers
- Firewalls dividing rooms and other parts of the factory
- General safety and security
- Environmental conservation
- Flammable materials stored underground
- Availability of fire-fighting equipment
- Two exits in every room
- Fire escapes
- Structural safety of walls, floors and roofs
- Protection against machinery

Production Costs

Functions of a cost accountant

- Consulting with the chief accountant to come to a decision on the spending of fixed and working capital so as to obtain an optimum return
- Investigating deviations from set standards and making corrective recommendations
- Compiling a comparison between the different production methods and presenting it to management
- Bookkeeping for all manufacturing expenditure and costs
- Analysing cost components
- Calculating cost price so that a selling price may be set

Why cost is important to the consumer

- The consumer has limited means or buying power.
- The consumer will benefit from a lower selling price.
- The consumer will benefit, too, in a market where supply and demand forces prices down.
- Competitive prices of substitute goods also benefit consumers.

Why cost is important to the manufacturer

- Provides management with information for decision-making
- Helps to determine the break-even point
- Determines the cost of raw materials, labour and other manufacturing costs for each component and completed product
- Makes easier the adjustment of the selling price for the purposes of competition

- Allows management to analyse unit production costs
- Determines safety margins in production

Cost components

- Direct raw material costs — costs of raw materials used to make a specific product.
- Direct labor costs — costs of labor used to make a specific product.
- Overheads — costs that cannot be charged directly to a specific product.
- Fixed overheads — stable costs that occur regardless of whether or not goods are being produced (i.e. rent of factory). These are allocated according to the number of machine hours.
- Variable overheads — changeable overhead costs that vary according to the number of goods produced (i.e. water and lights). These are allocated according to the number of labor hours.
- Indirect raw material costs — costs of raw materials whose role in the manufacturing of a product cannot be easily determined (i.e. glue).
- Indirect labor costs — costs of labour that cannot be charged to a particular product (i.e. the floor sweeper in a factory).

- Primary production costs = direct labour + direct raw materials
- Overhead expenses = fixed overheads + variable overheads
- Total production costs = primary production costs + overhead expenses

CASE STUDIES

With the changing expectations of customers, organisations constantly need to adapt to remain competitive. When faced with such pressures for change, managers may look for situations which are familiar to them.

This may involve improving the ways in which they operate, but only little by little. This is called incremental change. The danger is that improving little by little might not be enough. They need to adapt to all of the bigger changes in the environment of that business as well. If they don't, what happens is strategic drift.

Strategic Drift

When an organisation experiences strategic drift, it does not make strong and radical decisions to deal adequately with all of the changes in its business environment. To avoid strategic drift, managers within organisations have to embrace change fully. This means building a responsive organisation.

AEGON UK

This case study focuses upon AEGON in the UK, part of the AEGON Group, one of the world's largest life insurance and pensions companies. AEGON owns pensions, life insurance, asset management and adviser businesses in the UK. The case study illustrates the success that embracing and pursuing change has brought to AEGON in the UK. It is helping AEGON move towards its goal of becoming 'the best long-term savings and protection business within the UK'.

The AEGON Group has 27,000 employees and over 25 million customers worldwide. Its major markets are in the USA and Netherlands.

Since 1994, the UK has become another major and increasingly important market. In 1994 AEGON bought a large stake in Scottish Equitable. Scottish Equitable was a strong brand with a heritage that went back to the 1830s. Since then AEGON's UK business has grown both organically and by acquiring other businesses.

As most of the acquired companies kept their existing identities, awareness of AEGON in the UK remained relatively low. AEGON realised that such low levels of awareness could impact on its ability to achieve its ambitions. Therefore, it needed to combine the global strength of its parent with the experience and reputation of the domestic company brands, like Scottish Equitable, that made up AEGON in the UK.

External Factors Influencing Change

One of the main challenges for decision-makers is to understand the environment in which they are operating. They can then identify key issues which they need to respond to. Understanding these key issues improves decision-taking and reduces uncertainty. Few industries have experienced as many changes in their external environment in recent years as financial services.

Thinking ahead and saving for retirement is a concept that is sometimes difficult for people to understand. In the UK, life expectancy has risen in recent years so people can expect to be retired for longer.

In many instances, individuals have not planned properly for retirement and there may be a shortfall in the amount of money available. There is also a drive by the government to reduce dependency on the State in old age. Added to this many companies have introduced new, less expensive pension schemes or insisted on employee pension contributions where they did not in the past.

These factors mean people have to make decisions to invest properly at an earlier stage of their working lives. Investing in the future helps people to prepare in advance for old age. The benefits of such an investment are only realised years later.

The Industry

The life insurance and pensions industry, in which AEGON operates, has had a poor reputation in recent years. Some organisations have been accused of 'mis-selling' by not providing consumers with the best product for their needs. To prevent similar situations arising in the future, the Financial Services Authority (FSA) has put significant amounts of regulation on the industry.

Financial services products are often difficult to understand. People do not always feel equipped to choose between the range of financial products and services and are not sure where to seek support and advice.

In addition, falling values on the Stock Exchange have affected the investment return on some products, such as mortgage endowments. For some people this means that the product they bought has not delivered the financial return they expected. All this has created uncertainty in the financial services industry.

The industry has also been characterised by intense competition. AEGON is in competition with organisations which sell directly to consumers and which are better known in the UK. AEGON distributes its products and services to customers mainly through financial advisers. AEGON, as a reputable company, has had to address and overcome these industry-wide problems to remain competitive.

Reasons for Change

AEGON had historically been successful but government-imposed price controls had reduced profitability. Compared to its competitors, AEGON was not well known by consumers. It had developed good products and services and had a good reputation with distributors, particularly in the area of pensions which were a key strength of Scottish Equitable.

However, it was not as well recognised in areas other than pensions. Often these other areas, such as offshore investment products, were more profitable. If consumers are to invest in a product long term, they need to know more about the organisation they are dealing with. They need to recognise the brand and understand more about the brand values that it represents. As AEGON traded under a number of brand names it was not always easy for financial advisers and consumers to recognise the breadth and depth of the company in the UK.

How to Move Forward?

With a new Chief Executive (CEO) in place, AEGON underwent a discovery phase. The purpose of this was to find out what it had to do to meet the CEO's goal. This goal was to build 'the best long-term savings and protection business in the UK'. This time of discovery focused on three key questions:

1. What do we stand for in the UK?
2. What do we want to stand for in the UK?
3. What should we be doing about it?

Brand Audit

To answer these questions AEGON undertook a brand audit. This audit looked at two aspects:

- the company internally
- how the organisation was positioned externally.

The purpose of the audit was to find out more information about the organisation. This helped AEGON to provide a more informed approach to the decisions that were needed to start the process of change. The audit showed that AEGON was solidly placed within the market. Its staff were known for their considerable expertise, innovation and clarity of communication.

The external audit also helped to discover where AEGON was positioned in relation to its competitors. People who were aware of AEGON saw it as being a refreshing and different organisation. However, there was evidence that people were confused about the breadth of what AEGON did because it traded under a number of different company brands.

Creating a New Culture is a Key Part of the Change Process

Culture refers to the personality and attitude of an organisation. It also includes the shared beliefs, values and behaviour of the employees. These determine the ways in which the organisation and its people make decisions and solve problems.

The goal of AEGON's CEO helped to provide a vision for change. Financial objectives were important as the path for future developments depended upon these. It was also important to create more clarity about who AEGON was. With limited awareness of AEGON in the UK, it was important to explain what it had to offer, how big the organisation was within the UK and how strong it was globally.

At the heart of this strategy was the need to:

a) simplify financial services and provide more customer focus. It was important that consumers understood more precisely what they were buying, as well as the benefits and services they received

b) develop the workforce. The objective was to develop the skills needed within the business to help it change.

AEGON also created opportunities for progression from one job to another in a way that provided individuals with a coherent career path.

c) create a more distinct presence within the marketplace. This involved refreshing the AEGON brand in a way that made it more distinctive from its competitors and more attractive to customers.

A Behaviour Framework

In order to help embed this culture, AEGON developed a behaviour framework to support its brand values. This was designed to influence how people at all levels within the organisation could work and make decisions. These behaviours emphasise the values of the organisation. They have helped to build AEGON's culture and have also influenced its performance. AEGON also introduced a Management Development Programme, supported by a leading Management College.

The eight behaviours are:

- Think customer
- Embrace change
- Encourage excellence
- Act with integrity
- Decisive action
- Work together
- Learn and grow
- Relate and communicate.

'Think customer' is about 'ensuring that the customer's needs are at the heart of our business, informing actions, decisions and behaviours'. For senior managers this means keeping the customer's experience at the heart of what AEGON does. Other managers and professionals are encouraged to '*innovate with your customers in mind*'. All staff are encouraged to keep to commitments made to customers by doing '*what you say you will, when you say you will*'.

Implementing the Change

Before the change consumers were confused about who AEGON was, what it did and how it fitted together. The audit had shown that global scale was important but so was local expertise.

In the past, the AEGON brand had not been heavily promoted alongside Scottish Equitable or the other brands that it traded under. The brand strategy helped to reposition the brand within the industry.

Now the association with AEGON is much stronger. For example, Scottish Equitable is now AEGON Scottish Equitable -reflecting both local knowledge and global power. All the brands now carry a new common look which is refreshing and different. This, along with the values and behaviours, is helping to make the brand 'refreshingly different'.

Impacts of the Change

The changes affected the organisation both internally and externally. Within the organisation, they influenced not only how people behaved but also how they communicated. The organisation has become more focused on the customer. The emphasis is on making information clearer for the customer to understand and the company easier to do business with.

To help embed the values and behaviours, AEGON established a new relationship with Shirley Robertson, the famous yachtswoman and the only British female athlete to have won gold medals at consecutive Olympic Games. By associating AEGON with an individual who embodies similar values, it was able to bring the values and behaviours to life for staff.

However, AEGON had to develop the brand and its reputation. It did this is a number of ways:

- External promotional campaigns emphasised the relationship between Scottish Equitable and AEGON. This helped to reinforce the local knowledge and the global power of AEGON in the UK.
- The CEO talked to the media about the need for change. The refreshing of the brand internally and externally resulted in strong positive feedback.
- AEGON has launched new and innovative products. For example, the 5 for Life annuity has helped to change the way in which consumers can look at their retirement income. It provides more certainty about levels of income for the consumer, with AEGON providing the levels of return promised and being responsible for any risks associated with doing so.

Today the AEGON brand has a position from which it is influencing the financial services industry. It has posted record results with significant growth in underlying earnings. It has also increased its new business across a mix of profitable products and services, reflecting its continued strength.

Conclusion

Change is continuous. The process of change is a journey. External factors will always be there to influence business organisations.

AEGON responded to these factors by simplifying, clarifying and strengthening its brand in the UK.

As organisations change, their patterns of behaviour and business culture develop. For AEGON, this is a cycle in which the business uses its knowledge to learn from its experiences.

This has helped AEGON as an organisation to move positively towards achieving its full potential and to remain competitive in an increasingly difficult market.

AMWAY

Introduction

Corporate Social Responsibility (CSR) means businesses and organisations working responsibly and contributing positively to the communities they operate in. It involves working with employees, their families, the local community and society at large to improve their quality of life. Companies that operate in a socially responsible way strengthen their reputations. In business, reputation is everything. It determines the extent to which customers want to buy from you, partners are willing to work with you and your standing in the community.

The Company

Amway is one of the world's largest direct sales organisations with over 3 million Independent Business Owners (IBOs) in over 80 markets and territories worldwide. It is a family-owned business with a strong emphasis on family values. Its IBOs are often couples. Many of these are raising families. They therefore have a strong bond with children. These families are more than happy to partner with Amway, who, as part of its Corporate Social Responsibility strategy, works with UNICEF, the United Nations Children's Fund.

As a family company, Amway is committed to playing a part in improving the lives of children in need across the globe. In this way, the company is able to show its commitment to the support of global causes.

Amway defines a global cause as 'a social issue affecting many people around the world engaged in a struggle or plight that warrants a charitable response'.

This case study shows how Amway is a business that does more than provide customers with good quality products. It shows the practical realities of Amway's global commitment and how it plays a key role in the communities in which it operates.

Growth and Responsibility

An understanding of how Amway operates as an organisation gives a clearer picture of the contribution it can make to help children in need across the globe. Amway's vision is to help people live better lives. It does this every day by providing a low-cost low-risk business opportunity based on selling quality products.

What does Amway do?

Amway distributes a range of branded products. These products are sold to IBOs worldwide. The IBOs are Amway's links with consumers and the communities in which they operate. The IBOs are self-employed and are highly motivated. They work within the guidelines of Amway's Rules of Conduct and Code of Ethics, which are about being honest and responsible in trading. IBOs sell to people that they know or meet. They can introduce others to the Amway business.

Typical products that IBOs sell include:

- personal care – fragrances, body care
- skin care and cosmetics
- durables such as cookware and water treatment systems

- nutrition and wellness products such as food supplements, food and drinks.

IBOs play a key part in helping Amway to deliver its Global Cause Programme.

Amway Programmes

In order to give many of the world's children a chance to live a better life, Amway launched the global One by One campaign for children in 2003. The One by One programme:

- helps Amway to bring its vision to life
- declares what the company stands for
- builds trust and respect in Amway brands
- establishes Corporate Social Responsibility at a high level.

Amway encourages staff and IBOs to support its One by One campaign for children.

Since 2001, Amway Europe has been an official partner of UNICEF and has been able to contribute over □2 million (about £1.4 million). The focus is on supporting the worldwide 'Immunisation Plus' programme.

This involves, for example, providing measles vaccines to children across the globe. The 'Plus' is about using the vehicle of immunisation to deliver other life-saving services for children.

It is about making health systems stronger and promoting activities that help communities and families to improve child-care practices. For example the 'Plus' could include providing vitamin A supplements in countries where there is vitamin A deficiency.

Since 2001, Amway and its IBOs across Europe have been supporting UNICEF's child survival programme. The need is great. One out of ten children in Kenya does not live to see its fifth birthday, largely through preventable diseases. Malaria is the biggest killer with 93 deaths per day. Only 58% of children under two are fully immunised.

The work of the One by One programme is illustrated by a field trip undertaken by Amway IBOs to Kenya. The IBOs travelled to Kilifi in 2006 to meet children and to find out what the problems are in various communities. They act as champions spreading the message throughout their groups. In Kilifi, the focus is on trying to reach the most vulnerable children and pregnant mothers. The aim is to increase immunisation from 40% to 70%. Other elements of the programme involve seeking to prevent the transmission of HIV/AIDS to infants.

As the Amway organisation grows and prospers, it is able through CSR actions to help communities to grow and prosper too.

Developing a Strategy

A strategy is an organisational plan. Implementing a strategy involves putting that plan into action. In other words a strategy shows how a business will achieve its goals. The strategy thus enables an organisation to turn its values into action. Values are what a company stands for. An important value for Amway is being a caring company. Amway believes in demonstrating this caring approach and this is why it has partnered with UNICEF.

All Directors design strategies for the whole of an organisation. Effective strategies involve discussion and communication with others. The views of IBOs are influential in creating strategies for Amway. Amway's strategies for corporate social responsibility are cascaded through the organisation as shown below.

Amway's Global Cause strategy involves creating responsible plans that make a difference. However, the strategy is flexible. In shaping the strategy, research was carried out to find out which global causes IBOs support. The results showed that many favoured a cause that helped children. There was a clear fit between Amway's aims to help children and UNICEF's 'Immunisation Plus' programme for children.

Objectives

From the outset, Amway set out some clear objectives for its strategy. These were to:

- build loyalty and pride among IBOs and employees
- enhance Amway's reputation as a caring organisation
- make a real difference to human lives.

Child mortality is particularly high in developing countries because of infectious diseases. Many children could still be alive if they had been vaccinated.

For under £12 a child can be vaccinated against these diseases and has a fighting chance to reach adulthood. UNICEF's world child 'Immunisation Plus' programme is a fitting focus for the activities of Amway UK and its IBOs.

The UK initiative is part of a European-wide fundraising campaign for children. It recognises the importance of building good working relationships with UNICEF in each market in order to launch fundraising programmes through Amway's IBOs and their customers. The objective is to raise □500,000 (about £350,000) every year until 2010 across Amway Europe.

In 2005 Amway UK's partnership was deepened through becoming an official Corporate Partner of UNICEF UK. The Corporate Partnership is a closer longer-term relationship which benefits both partners. Working together the two parties raise money for UNICEF.

Identifying Stakeholders

Amway's Corporate Social Responsibility strategy has been developed with the interests of the following stakeholders in mind:

Communicating the Strategy

Good, clear communication is essential in making sure that the CSR strategy relates directly to the company business objectives. Communication also helps in putting the strategy into practice.

A number of communications media are used:

1. *Face-to-face communication*: Regular meetings take place between UNICEF, Amway and its IBOs. Through meetings with UNICEF staff, Amway is able to discuss the vision and objectives. It then passes the message on by meeting with IBOs. In 2005 the two organisations arranged a joint briefing day for IBO Leaders. They were able to hear firsthand experiences from UNICEF staff about their roles and UNICEF's work as well as where the money goes.
2. *Printed material*: Amway produces a monthly magazine for all IBOs called Amagram.
3. *Public relations materials* are also important, particularly at launch events for the initiative (e.g. in Milton Keynes in 2006).
4. *Email communication*: Email is very important in the company – it plays a significant part in keeping IBOs up-to-date.
5. *Online activities*: There is a micro-site dedicated to the Amway UK/UNICEF partnership on the UNICEF UK website.

FUNDRAISING

Amway Europe provides support for fundraising to the extent of □500,000 (about £350,000) per year through selling items such as:

- greetings cards
- multi-cultural gifts and cards
- stationery and wrapping paper
- toys for children.

However, Amway UK's support goes well beyond these activities. In addition, it involves staff fundraising events and raffles organised by the IBOs. UNICEF attends IBO major events (usually supported by 1,000 or more IBOs) where requested. A UNICEF stand outlines the work with speakers, literature and merchandise.

CONCLUSION

Amway is a family business with family values. Its IBOs are people who want to make a difference to the communities in which they operate and to the wider world community. This is Corporate Social Responsibility (CSR) in action.

The clue to Amway's success is the careful planning of its strategy and its involvement with many stakeholders in getting the strategy right. Of course, it is early days in the latest chapter of a strong relationship between Amway and UNICEF. Evaluation is taking place to measure the success of the initiative in terms of meeting fundraising goals. Customer research is carried out to test customers' views on the relationship and to find out how aware the general public is about what Amway is doing in the field of CSR.

4

Social and Environmental Responsibility

INTRODUCTION

Businesses help society to prosper. They do so by providing goods and services that consumers want. Businesses also contribute to the well-being of society. They provide jobs and incomes, they innovate and build the skills of their employees and pay taxes to support government spending. They provide returns to shareholders and shareholder funds that generate incomes for pensioners.

Anglo American is one of the largest British-based international businesses and is one of the 20 largest companies on the London Stock Exchange. Chiefly through Tarmac, it employs nearly 8,000 people in the UK. It is also one of the world's largest mining companies. It has managed operations in over 40 countries and employs over 100,000 people worldwide.

Anglo American produces five main materials:

It also owns a 45% non-managing stake in diamond leader, De Beers.

Most of Anglo American's work is in primary industry. Primary industry is the first stage of industrial activity. For Anglo American this mainly means extracting materials from the ground through mining and quarrying. To produce metals like copper or platinum it then processes the ore.

These materials turn into manufactured goods at the secondary stage of production. For example, coal and iron become steel at a steel works. Finished steel goes into many industrial products. These include steel for ships' hulls, car bodies, bridges or buildings.

Anglo American seeks to contribute to sustainable development through being socially and environmentally responsible. It achieves this through high performance in five overlapping areas.

Sustainable Development

Sustainable development is "passing on to future generations a stock of 'capital' that is at least as great as the one our generation inherited".

Sustainable development is based on respect for:

- one another, everyone who shares our planet
- future generations (what is called 'inter-generational equity'), as well as the existing one
- for nature itself – for plants, animals and all life forms.

Exploitation of natural resources is essential for economic growth. For many poorer, developing countries, the development of these resources is the only means of attracting foreign investment and wider development. This in turn helps to fight poverty.

We all use natural resources. For example in:

- heating our homes
- travelling to work or school

- leisure activities (e.g. gym equipment has metal components).

Anglo American is a major provider of raw materials. To support sustainability, it must try to balance using 'natural' capital, such as iron ore, with activities that enhance skills, opportunities, health and education for local people. These may benefit them directly through community projects or indirectly through paying taxes and royalties.

Sustainable Development Priniciples

Anglo American has created a set of sustainable development principles that underpin the way it seeks to do business. These are to:

- be ethical, efficient and create value for its stakeholders
- create meaningful employment in safe, healthy environments
- reduce its environmental footprint and contribute to biodiversity
- increase innovation, technology and process improvement
- contribute towards building more adaptable societies in the communities where it operates.

Sustainability Programmes

The following examples illustrate how these principles work in practice.

Anglo American places a strong emphasis on Safety and Health. The mining industry has major safety challenges, including a substantial number of fatalities. Anglo American is seeking to address these through creating a 'zero mindset'. This means that the total elimination of accidents and injury is the goal. There is a supporting principle of 'zero repeats'. If an accident occurs, it should never happen again. All employees are expected to follow these rules. They are simple and non-negotiable standards.

Anglo American works in a number of countries where water is scarce, including Chile, Australia and South Africa. The Emalahleni water treatment plant in South Africa purifies waste water from coal mines into drinking water for use by the Emalahleni community.

At the Kleinkopje colliery in South Africa water from mining activity is treated and used for farming projects such as growing beans. In the UK, Tarmac avoids using water from drinkable sources. Instead, it uses water resulting from industrial processes wherever possible.

It is important to note that Anglo American works in partnership to achieve many of its projects. This means it works with both governments and private companies, and with community groups or international donors to ensure that the capacities and networks of local communities are enhanced.

In South Africa Anglo American has the largest directly delivered workplace HIV/AIDS treatment programmes in the world. It took the lead in providing medical help for its HIV employees at a time when the government was not prepared to provide life-saving drugs. It provides free drugs to about 4,500 employees as well as extensive community prevention and treatment programmes.

Anglo American sees technology transfer and capacity building as significant elements in helping local communities to grow economically. In Venezuela, it has created experimental farms for the transfer of horticultural and agricultural knowledge.

In Chile, it has worked with goat farmers and beekeepers to improve techniques and product marketing. In South

Africa and Chile, the company's programmes generate new small businesses through supply chain opportunities, training, mentoring and access to finance.

Anglo American and Sustainable Development

Anglo American reviews how it operates in a sustainable way in a number of areas.

In practice:

1. Anglo American carries out its mining with a concern to:
   - minimise noise and other types of pollution
   - minimise harm to the landscape after mining has been completed
   - seek to improve the skills and opportunities available to local people.
2. Anglo American is active in many conservation projects. These developments surround all of its plants. At Tarmac's Langford Quarry in the UK, the company has created reed beds in streams and ponds surrounding the quarry. Reed beds are an endangered habitat in this country. Members of the local community worked with Tarmac to plant the first 10,000 reeds.

   Anglo American seeks to contribute financially to local communities where it operates.
3. The company believes that mining should become a catalyst for wider development. Anglo American takes part in a range of such projects, including helping to generate new small businesses. These help local farmers and businesses to prosper. It contributes to health education and schooling programmes too. These take place within the communities in which it works.

Anglo American was named as the mining sector leader for 2005 in the Dow Jones Sustainability Index.

This index was launched in 1999 to track the financial performance of the leading sustainability-driven companies worldwide. Anglo American also won the Business in the Community International Award in 2005. This was for its contribution to the Millennium Development Goals in Africa.

The pressure for social and environmental responsibility.

Pressure for social and environmental responsibility comes from two main sources:

- internal to the business
- external to the business.

Internal Pressures

Internal pressures are the most important ones in driving change. The decision-makers in Anglo American ensure it works towards sustainability. The Board of Directors has identified key strategic issues for the business. These include:

The Board establishes the key principles for using resources in the most efficient way. The business must work closely with local communities. It must also minimise the impact of its operations on the environment. Anglo American has created a series of policies and plans that put principles into action.

Shareholders are the owners of Anglo American and want the business to do well long-term. They recognise that stability, prosperity and community confidence are important in sustaining the business. These factors help to persuade other communities that mining can be compatible with a decent environment and social progress.

Another internal pressure comes from the company's need to recruit talented new staff and retain valued employees. Anglo American aims to attract and retain the services of the most appropriately skilled individuals.

It relies on the skills, enthusiasm and commitment of its people to meet the needs of the business and to fulfill its aims and objectives. By showing it behaves responsibly with regard to the environment and the communities it works in, it can attract the widest range of people to the organisation.

External Pressures

External pressures are also important. For example, legislation plays a part. The UK Parliament provides minimum standards for areas such as the treatment of workers, the environment and customers. Because they have an international reputation to protect, major multinational companies will generally seek to operate within the law. In almost all countries, governments are also the ultimate owner of mineral rights and provide a mining business with its licence to operate. In some developing countries, however, governments promote laws, but do not have the mechanisms to enforce them.

Meeting International Standards

Anglo American also seeks to meet the increasing requirements of a number of international standards initiatives, including:

There are significant business pressures for behaving responsibly. Prosperous and stable communities support long-term business success. This leads to better returns for shareholders.

- the ten principles of the United Nations Global Compact. The governments of the thirty or so leading developed countries (the Organisation for Economic Co-operation and Development (OECD) have also adopted a set of guidelines. Multinational companies are expected to comply with these wherever they operate. There is a complaints process led by governments to support the guidelines.

- the International Labour Organisation has agreed guidelines for companies for the treatment of employees and contractors
- a number of initiatives which involve governments, NGOs and businesses working together voluntarily on issues like governance and human rights. Anglo American is party to two of these groupings whose guiding principles have become standards in practice– the Voluntary Principles on Security and Human Rights and the Extractive Industries Transparency Initiative.

Strong pressure in some markets may come from customers. Many customers demand high standards of ethical behaviour. There are also pressure groups such as the World Wide Fund for Nature (WWF), Oxfam or Amnesty, which seek to ensure that businesses operate ethically and in a sustainable way.

IMPACTS ON AND BENEFITS TO BUSINESS

There are real benefits to a business in acting responsibly. Being responsible wins the trust of communities. It gains respect from the governments of countries where it operates. It wins the loyalty of customers and the respect of the public. It gives a company an edge in attracting new recruits and talent. It wins recognition from investors for managing a business well.

Anglo American has made sure that its social and investment programmes match its strategic objective of being a good citizen. Today it is common practice to refer to the Triple Bottom Line of a business. A business is successful if it makes a financial profit on the bottom line. To continually generate profits, it is also necessary that:

a) a business respects the environment and

b) takes a wider social responsibility.

SHARING ECONOMIC BENEFITS

It is important to understand how the benefits of an international company such as Anglo American are distributed amongst its various stakeholders. A relatively small proportion of its 'value added' will typically go directly to shareholders with suppliers, employees, governments and lenders also benefiting significantly.

Anglo American has created an innovative process -the Socio-Economic Assessment Toolbox (SEAT). This measures the impact of all its activities on the communities in which it operates.

It engages local stakeholders in each community to learn about their concerns, needs and priorities. It then sets out its plans for improving its socio-economic performance through a three-year action plan made widely available to local people. SEAT enables the company to generate a successful triple bottom line.

Social and environmental responsibilities are vital components of a business strategy. They are the cornerstones of successful sustainable businesses.

Anglo American today has a strong reputation in many countries.

This reputation comes from basing strategic decision-making on respected social and environmental principles. This starts with senior managers and is carried through right down to grass roots community projects.

FLEXIBLE WORKING PATTERNS AT THE AUDIT COMMISSION

Today's working world is dramatically different from that of the past. Charles Handy in his book, *The Future of Work* (1984), warned that the old patterns of work were breaking down and that new ways of working were on their way. He was right. Handy believed that modern organisations need to be flexible so that they can adapt quickly to the changing pressures that they face.

Advances in information and communications technologies have helped many businesses to:

- provide opportunities for the business to become a more inclusive employer through the development of homeworking
- motivate workers through more flexible work practices.

This case study shows how the Audit Commission has developed and implemented flexible work practices to improve its services and meet the changing needs of its staff.

WHAT DOES THE AUDIT COMMISSION DO?

The Audit Commission is an independent body that is accountable to the Office of the Deputy Prime Minister (ODPM).

The work of the Audit Commission is varied. An 'audit' has two main elements. It involves:

i. a formal examination of a set of accounts to see if they are true and fair

ii. a checking of quality and efficiency.

The Audit Commission investigates services in the public sector. The finance for these services comes from taxes and other sources. It ensures that this money is used properly.

The range of services audited by the Audit Commission includes:

- the criminal justice system
- local government
- the National Health Service.

The Audit Commission inspects the operations of these public services to find out how each service is performing. The advice that is given following an audit helps to provide better value for money that comes from taxation and better services for the public.

Business Activity

Those who work for an organisation need to know where they are going.

This is often expressed in a mission statement. The mission of the Audit Commission is '*to be a driving force in the improvement of public services. We promote good practice and help those responsible for public services to achieve better outcomes for citizens, with a focus on those people who need public services most.*'

Within the Audit Commission, there are many different jobs with varying levels of duties. Junior posts are involved with a range of administrative duties. The next level involves supervisory posts where they could be managing teams of people.

Job roles within the Audit Commission fall into three different families or groups of jobs:

- audit family
- performance audit family
- functional family.

Audit Family

Those in the audit family are involved in carrying out financial audits. Most of these auditors will have professional accounting qualifications.

Each team of auditors will visit clients such as local authorities or police services to carry out complex audits.

Performance Audit Family

The people working in the performance audit family will have worked in the public sector and have direct experience of running public services.

They use their experience to help public sectors managers improve the efficiency of their organisations.

Functional Family

The functional family includes many others who help to ensure that the core business is run well.

These people work in research posts, internal finance, human resources, information technology, communications and the legal department.

Types of Employment

The Audit Commission is regularly faced with changing employment needs. A number of different patterns of employment have been developed to meet these needs.

These include:

- full-time employees
- part-time employees
- job-sharing arrangements
- permanent and fixed term posts
- the use of temps or contractors from agencies.

These different contracts help the Audit Commission to cope with all of its changing needs. They also help it to be flexible. There are three main types of flexibility:

- numerical flexibility
- functional flexibility
- place-of-work flexibility.

Numerical Flexibility

The Audit Commission is constantly faced with peaks and troughs in the workload that cannot be met simply by having its employees on full-time contracts.

There are situations where they need either more staff or fewer staff. By increasing or reducing staff in these situations the Audit Commission has developed numerical flexibility.

Functional Flexibility

The Audit Commission has also developed flexibility through developing the skills of its employees to deal with a wider variety of work. This means that when the nature and type of work changes, employees are comfortable undertaking different tasks. This is known as functional flexibility.

Place-of-work Flexibility

Homeworking is an example of place-of-work flexibility. The Audit Commission uses this way to respond to the challenges within their business environment. This method of working has helped it to meet more closely the needs of its staff.

As part of its flexible working arrangements, homeworking has helped to transform the ways in which many people work and improve their work-life balance.

Homeworking

Homeworking occurs where an employee uses her or his home as a work base. There are two main types of homeworking:

1. *Occasional homeworking* – the employee may work sometimes from home, but is normally present at an Audit Commission office or working on the site of a client for the majority of their working time. They still have an office base.
2. *Regular homeworking* – the employee works from home for the majority of the time.

Homeworking involves one-off set-up costs in which a home is provided with access to broadband and information and communications technology equipment.

There are also the ongoing costs of using these technologies.

In the same way that health and safety is important in the workplace, it is also important in the home. A risk assessment of health and safety issues is undertaken to ensure that the work area is suitable.

THE BENEFITS OF MANAGING A FLEXIBLE WORKFORCE

For regular homeworking to take place, it has to be appropriate to the working needs of the Audit Commission. An employee wanting to work from home has to apply to do so.

He or she must show managers how their work from home would affect customers, colleagues and the people they manage or work with. After the homeworking arrangement is set up, it is regularly reviewed. This monitors its effectiveness for both the employee and the Audit Commission.

ADVANTAGES OF HOMEWORKING

The advantages to employees and the business are very strong. For example, the Audit Commission's corporate offices are based in Millbank in London. There are many reasons for employees based there to want to adopt homeworking. The following outline some of the main ones:

- The trip into the city can take up to two hours each way on the train.
- People may have childminding arrangements to set up and pay for.

Regular homeworking helps an organisation to develop family-friendly policies that improve the work-life balance of its staff.

- Some may have considered a break from work while their children are young.

For the organisation, homeworking assists in recruiting individuals who are attracted to this style of working and this enables the Audit Commission to retain a diverse workforce. The process is inclusive as it takes account of the wider needs of employees.

Other Benefits

The other benefits of homeworking are that it:

- reduces travelling and this is good for the environment
- frees up desk space and allows office accommodation to be used more efficiently
- uses information and communications technologies to good effect.

MANAGEMENT SYSTEMS FOR EFFECTIVE FLEXIBLE WORKING

The Audit Commission has a system of matrix management. This is a system in which individuals work in teams that are not necessarily supervised by their own line manager. These project teams are not functional, but may include staff from across the three job families.

Whoever manages the team will also manage the homeworker.

Each person may work on a number of projects for a number of different teams. In this type of homeworking situation, individuals manage their own role and also undertake the responsibilities for each team they work with.

Problems with homeworking

Homeworking clearly involves an element of trust. The challenge is to keep everybody informed about what is happening within the business. The intranet has a key role in doing this.

There are several problems associated with homeworking but the Audit Commission has worked hard at minimising the effects of these on its staff. The main ones are:

i. Not mixing with colleagues. Individuals may lose the office culture because the reliance on technology means that relationships become impersonal. To overcome this, the Audit Commission arranges training events and awaydays, as well as networking opportunities and staff conferences.

ii. Homeworkers become dependent upon the technologies. If there is a power cut or a computer problem, then this could affect the work.

iii. Health & safety risks and keeping confidential files at home.

The Audit Commission sets out clear guidelines as part of its homeworking policy. These guidelines refer to employers' liability insurance which covers employees while they are working from home. The guidelines also refer to confidential files that may be kept for a temporary period within the home.

Homeworkers have to balance both their work and their domestic responsibilities.

The arguments for and against homeworking depend upon a high degree of trust.

This is because an employee is working independently outside the office. In a team-based environment, each individual needs to be available to other members of the team as and when they are needed. Being able to set their own goals and identify their priorities is important for homeworkers.

In a competitive environment change is considered normal.

Organisations have to be flexible.This flexibility involves looking at the workforce and workforce practices to identify new and better ways of responding to these different needs.

Sometimes flexibility involves employing individuals with different sorts of contracts. Flexibility also involves staff developing a wider variety of skills that they can use across a range of different types of work.

This case study emphasises how the Audit Commission has adopted a range of flexible working practices to good effect. Using homeworking provides flexibility for the organisation and enables it to include people who might otherwise find it difficult to work for the Audit Commission.

By being inclusive the Audit Commission has retained its staff in a way that helps them to support their work-life balance.

HOW MARKET RESEARCH SUPPORTS THE NEW PRODUCT DEVELOPMENT PROCESS

Market research is the process by which businesses find out about customers' needs, wants and desires. It makes possible the successful development of new products.

This study shows how an international company, Beiersdorf, combines market research with new product development on its NIVEA Deodorant brand to provide exciting new products that better meet consumer requirements.

Beiersdorf has a clear goal -to be as close as possible to consumers, regardless of which country they live in. Developing superior consumer insights is fundamental to the continued future success of Beiersdorf and its international brands like NIVEA, Eucerin and Atrixo.

These are the result of more than 120 years of experience in research and development.

Beiersdorf has launched many new brands and products into a variety of countries and categories.

Being an innovation leader has allowed Beiersdorf actively to shape its markets and set new trends. These product launches have led to long-term global growth.

The Key Stages of Market Research and New Product Development

Market research involves the systematic gathering, recording and analyzing of data about customers, competitors and the market. This links marketers to consumers by supplying essential information to solve marketing challenges and help with marketing decisions.

Market research helps a company create and develop an up-to-date and relevant portfolio of products.

Creating New Products

Beiersdorf's international Market Research team is based at company headquarters in Hamburg, Germany. The team's objective is to be the voice of the consumers within the organisation. High-quality market research has helped secure the long-term future of the business. Analysing and understanding the data gathered on consumers' behaviours, needs, attitudes and opinions minimises the risks involved in making marketing decisions.

Market research in a global organisation needs the help and support of the company's overseas affiliate companies. Most affiliate companies (in the UK for example) have dedicated Market Research Managers. They help the central research team in gathering and interpreting consumer views. These views provide information or insights that ultimately result in the development of new products suitable for a global market.

This case study follows the development of a new NIVEA Deodorant called Pearl and Beauty aimed at young women. This case study will give you a clear picture of how market research has helped New Product Development (NPD).

Identifying consumer insights and product needs -where to start?

Market research should start with the consumer and serves two purposes:

1) To inform companies about consumer needs and desires. What are the trends in the market? What do consumers want?
2) To give consumers the opportunity to talk to the providers of products and services so that their views are taken into account.

Businesses exist in a fast-moving world with increased consumer choice. It is essential that a company knows its market and its consumers before developing any new product. Lots of questions need answering.

Consumer insights drive New Product Development. This information takes into account their behaviours, attitudes and beliefs. It is an expression of their wishes and desires. Businesses use consumer insights to create opportunities for their brands. It is the starting point that enables brands to fit meaningfully into consumers' lives.

Across countries, consumers are different in terms of culture and lifestyle. NIVEA's challenge was to find similar insights from consumers across different countries. This was used to optimize product development.

Secondary Research

In the deodorant category, NIVEA used many secondary research sources to discover consumers' views and their need for deodorants. These related to different markets and were supplied by local country market researchers. These included:

i. A consumer Usage and Attitude study. This had been conducted a few years earlier across various markets (UK, France and USA).

ii. An external study by Fragrance Houses. This covered the importance of scent and fragrance to people's well-being and mood.

Primary Research

The research team felt therefore there was not enough recent knowledge about the consumer in the secondary research. They commissioned some primary qualitative research in key markets (Germany, France, UK and USA). This was aided by the local Market Research Manager. The aim was to understand the motivations for using deodorant amongst the female consumer.

Primary research is used when there is no existing data available to answer your questions.

The research involved small discussion groups of females. This helped researchers understand the beliefs and motivations of this group. There were several main findings:

There is steady growth in females shaving. They wanted to look after their underarms throughout all seasons (not just in summer).

Women cared increasingly about the condition of their underarms.

Women desired attractive, neat underarms. This symbolised sensuality and femininity.

The deodorant segment remained focused on functional rather than beautifying products.

Results of the Research

The market research revealed an unexplored market potential for NIVEA Deodorant. The brand did not have a specific product that addressed 'underarm beauty' for the female consumer. No direct competitor was offering a product to meet these needs.

So there was a clear opportunity to develop a new product. This would fit across different markets and with the current NIVEA Deodorant range.

Turning Consumer Insights into Product Concepts

Consumers showed a need for a 'beautifying, caring deodorant'. The team generated ideas on how to address the consumer need.

From these ideas the marketing team created 'product concepts'. These describe the product benefits and how they will meet the consumer needs. Several concepts were written in different ways. These explained and expressed unique product attributes.

The company needed to know which concept was preferred by prospective consumers. It carried out market research to test whether the concepts would work.

The research was conducted amongst the desired target market. For Pearl and Beauty, the desired target market was 18-35 year-old women who were beauty-orientated, followed fashion and looked for products with extra benefits.

Quantitative research on the concept was carried out in two test markets (France and Germany). An international company like Beiersdorf must test products in more than one market to assess properly the global appeal.

The concepts were tested monadically. Monadic testing means that the respondent of the test is only shown one concept. This stops the respondent being biased by seeing many variations of the same product concept.

A number of criteria were used to test the concepts:

1) Deodorant category performance measures. These included wetness, dryness, and fragrance. The new concept must deliver generic core benefits.
2) Product attributes specific to the new product and NIVEA core values. The new Pearl and Beauty product has additional benefits to a 'regular' deodorant. For example, it leaves your skin feeling silky and gives you beautiful underarms. Consumers needed to understand and see these benefits.
3) The product needed to be relevant and motivate a consumer to purchase it.

The team chose the 'winning' concept. This best conveyed beauty while remaining relevant to the deodorant category and NIVEA brand.

Next the research team tested various name ideas for the product and developed different designs for the packaging.

Packaging design plays a very important role in helping to communicate the image of the product. Pearl and Beauty needed to communicate femininity and sophistication. Pink was a natural colour choice for the packaging. They also used a soft pearlescent container to emphasise the 'pearl extracts' in the product.

Various design ideas were tested using quantitative market research. In addition, this helped to predict the volume of the new products that would be sold, the optimal selling price and the level of switching from existing NIVEA Deodorant and competitor products.

TESTING THE PRODUCT, BRAND POSITIONING AND ADVERTISING

Testing

The stages described so far produced a product concept that consumers felt was relevant and which they were willing to buy. The next stage was to test the product on actual customers. Many product launches fail, despite great advertising. A big reason is because the product fails to live up to the promises made.

The Market Research Team conducted a product usage test. A de-branded sample of the proposed new product was given to the target consumer of females in several countries. De-branded means the deodorant was in a blank container so that the consumers did not know who made the product or what type it was.

Very often consumers form opinions about products and services from advertising and packaging. This can sometimes be very strong and creates a bias in what they think of a product before trying it.

The consumers were asked to use the new deodorant for a week. They kept a diary of when they used it and scored the performance of the deodorant against a list of criteria. These included:

- Did it keep you dry all day?
- Did you have to reapply it?
- Did you like the fragrance?
- Did it last all day?
- Was the deodorant reliable?

Consumers applied the 'de-branded' deodorant under their right armpit and continued to use their current deodorant under their left armpit. This helped the users gauge if it was as good as or better than the brand they normally used. This gave a measure of how likely the consumer would be to swap brands.

The results of the test were very positive. Most consumers loved the fragrance and the feel of the product on their skin. They felt it performed as well as their current deodorant. Most said they would swap their brands after trying the product.

Brand Positioning

Now the marketing team had a new product idea that consumers liked. It had a name and packaging design that were well received. They now needed to check how this fitted with the rest of the NIVEA Deodorant brand positioning and range.

The brand position is the specific niche in the market that the brand defines itself as occupying.

The NIVEA Deodorant Pearl and Beauty adds a touch of feminine sophistication and elegance to the NIVEA Deodorant brand's personality. This built on the core deodorant positioning. It made NIVEA Deodorant more appealing, modern and unique to trendy, young female consumers.

USING QUALITATIVE RESEARCH TO INFORM ADVERTISING

The next stage was to brief an advertising agency to develop communication to support the launch of the new product. Through market research the team could check whether the advertisements positively supported and communicated the new product.

The company conducted qualitative research on some advertising ideas amongst various groups of the target consumers. It presented ideas in the form of 'storyboards' of what a TV advert could look like. The objective was to evaluate which were the best ideas in terms of:

- Did they stand out as exciting or different?
- Were they relevant to the consumer?
- Did they communicate the right things about the new product?
- Did they persuade the consumer to want to purchase the product?

EVALUATING SUCCESS

Once the product is launched and the consumer can actually purchase it, the research process does not stop.

Continuous consumer tracking can be carried out to find out consumers' views of the new product. This involves interviewing people every day to find out whether they are using the product, what they think of it and why they would purchase it.

Beiersdorf uses other, secondary data sources such as consumer panel data and EPOS (electronic point of sale) data. These monitor the sales effectiveness of the product throughout the launch phase and through the product life cycle.

CONCLUSION

New product development should start with an insight based on consumer needs.

Throughout the NPD process, market research is a valuable tool for Beiersdorf to check viability and minimise the risk of the product launches.

Being an international company, it is essential that Beiersdorf develops new products using the insights of consumers across markets and cultures. This ensures the products are relevant to a large number of global consumers and will deliver the maximum return when launched.

This maximises return on investment for the company and results in happy, satisfied and loyal consumers.

5

Creating World Class Quality Standards

INTRODUCTION

Successful businesses meet customer requirements. Customers expect products and services to meet certain standards and a Standard is a document that gives guidance on achieving this. It acts as a set of rules or guidelines for everyone involved in producing goods, managing a process or delivering a service.

BSI was the pioneer in creating quality and safety standards. It is the UK's National Standards Body and was the world's first.

BSI also plays a prominent role in the development of global standards. It:

- leads in the creation of standards
- tests and certifies products and services
- is one of the organisations that assesses Quality Management Systems (QMS).

Businesses gain an advantage over rivals by producing high quality goods and services that clearly meet standards. The standards are based on agreed best practice, for example, in handling environmental waste or meeting safety standards.

Businesses across the globe seek to meet international standards.

For example, an engineering company in the Far East might use international standards for its components and finished items. These show the world that its products meet this international standard and that it is willing to take part in global manufacture and trade.

There are thousands of standards available for businesses to choose to use, depending on the type of sector the business is operating in. There are standards for education, transport, health, retailing and many more sectors.

Standards help organisations to achieve safe and quality products, and services to meet their needs and those of their customers. For example, in a nursery school, parents would want to know that equipment such as climbing frames and bouncy castles meet the required safety standards. Therefore, manufacturers of these products would want to follow the appropriate standards.

What is Quality?

Quality is defined by the customer. A quality product or service meets customer requirements. Not all customers have the same requirements.

Two products may both be seen as quality products by their different users. For example, a village football team might be happy with a good football that they can kick around in a Sunday afternoon fixture. In contrast, the England football team would require a football that was up to international football (FIFA) standards. Quality can therefore be defined as being fit for the customer's purpose.

The most successful organisations are those that give customers what they want. Satisfied customers are loyal to those companies they feel best understand their requirements. As a result, they make repeat purchases and often recommend a business to their friends.

Organisations that meet standards in everything they do are most likely to give their customers the required quality. This is why a Quality Management System is so important. Quality Management is the process of managing quality at every stage within an organisation and commitment to it begins with the senior managers.

Every organisation would like to improve the way it operates.

A quality management framework helps an organisation to improve all its operations and helps to ensure it can maintain its ability continually to improve its performance.

Best Practice

BSI helps organisations to identify best practice in the manufacture of materials or products and translate this practice into standards.

For example, standards for sports equipment, such as basketball goal posts, highlight the need to use the most suitable materials and fixtures in the equipment. BSI works with industry specialists to identify best practices.

Currently BSI publishes almost 20,000 standards and each year adds 2,000 new or revised standards to the list.

Why are Standards Important?

There are a number of levels of standards creation.

The highest level – International Standards – is the most complex. It requires the widest level of agreement between those creating the standards. These standards have to satisfy the needs of the different groups represented, such as industrial, trade and consumer groups of all of the countries involved. These international standards, which are identified by the letters ISO, are most widely recognised across the globe.

ISO is an international standard and applies in most countries.

EN is a European Standard and is used throughout the countries of the European Union.

BS means the Standard is a British Standard.

A good example of an international standard relates to the format of credit cards.

Standard number BS EN ISO 7810: 1996 defines their dimensions. Keeping to this Standard is important as it means that people can use the cards worldwide. A traveller without cash in another country can be confident they can get money using their own card.

As a customer, you will have a lot more confidence in products you know have been tested and meet British, European and International Standards. In the same way, your school will want to purchase gym and science lab equipment that meets the specifications of the safety standards.

Benefits of Meeting Standards

Businesses therefore benefit from working with BSI to meet standards, because:

- standards protect consumers' fundamental right to safety, the right to be informed and the right to choose. These rights relate to products, services, processes and materials
- standardization promotes effective research and development, and makes products easier to use
- standardization relies on all sections of society being involved in standards. This provides an opportunity

for everyone to share knowledge and make their voice heard.

Competitive Advantage

A focus on quality also delivers competitive advantage.

Many businesses cannot compete by lowering prices because their market, for example, clothes or food, is very competitive. Therefore, they compete on quality. This means they deliver quality products at the right time to fit their customers' needs. Companies that focus on quality can compete against rivals who have lower cost bases.

Quality Products

A quality product is one that meets the requirements of its user. For example, a motorcyclist would want to purchase a helmet that had met tough road safety tests.

BSI is an independent, non-governmental organisation that offers product testing and certification services as part of its business.

BSI works with many different types of organisations, including commercial and private companies, government bodies and trade associations. It helps these organisations produce safe and quality products that meet the safety and quality requirements of the countries in which they are to be sold.

Countries around the world have different requirements that products and services have to meet in order for them to be legally sold or delivered. This means that BSI offers access to these markets for their customers.

For example, in the motor vehicle industry, certificates are required by European bodies for a variety of components for new road vehicles. BSI helps UK motor manufacturers by testing and certifying that their products meet the required standards. Some of the products that BSI tests for the UK motor industry include vehicle lighting, vehicle glass, motor cycle helmets and electronic equipment.

BSI Kitemark

BSI is also the owner and operator of the well-known Kitemark. This is an independent and highly recognised symbol of trust and safety in the UK and some countries around the world.

BSI runs a number of Kitemark schemes for various products and services as wide-ranging as lighting, fire extinguishers, 13 Amp plugs and motor cycle helmets.

The Kitemark schemes are voluntary, so it is the manufacturer or service provider's choice to go through the assessment process to gain the Kitemark. This clearly demonstrates that the manufacturer or service provider is committed to delivering a safe and quality product that meets the standards set.

The Kitemark is the symbol that gives consumers the assurance that the product conforms to the appropriate British, European or International Standard.

A Kitemark means BSI has independently tested the product and that it conforms to or exceeds the criteria of the relevant British Standard. BSI issues a BSI Kitemark license to the company to use the Kitemark.

The manufacturer pays for this service. This is only the start of the Kitemark process. The product is tested and the manufacturing process is assessed at regular intervals following the issue of the license.

The Kitemark is the symbol that gives consumers the assurance that the product conforms to the appropriate British, European or International Standard. It should therefore be safe and reliable. Manufacturers do not by law have to display a Kitemark on their products, but many do because it encourages consumers to buy and demonstrates the company's commitment to producing safe quality products.

CE Marking

Many products, such as new toys, must meet legal requirements before they can be sold within the European Community. These must carry CE marking. CE marking on a product is a manufacturer's claim that it meets all the requirements of the European legislation.

Some products carry both a Kitemark and CE marking but the two symbols indicate different degrees of certification.

Quality Processes

Businesses that work with international standards can create quality systems covering every aspect of their business.

For example, a number of organisations work with BSI to create Quality Management Systems (QMS). To achieve ISO 9001, organisations must meet eight quality management principles. These include:

- customer focus
- leadership – commitment to quality by the leaders of the organisation
- involvement of people – everyone in the organisation has a part to play
- making sure that those processes which create quality are identified
- continual improvement of the system.

When the organisation feels confident it is meeting the standard, it informs an assessor. The assessor will assess the effectiveness of the QMS. If it meets the standard a certificate will be awarded. This is subject to regular reviews. As well as building internal systems (inside the organisation), external systems (such as suppliers) must also meet quality standards.

The Supply Chain

Today, many businesses have long supply chains. This means they may source materials, parts and finished goods from across the globe.

For example, consider a modern plasma screen television. Some of the components may come from India, others from China or Eastern European countries. These separate components are put together into a sub-assembly i.e. part of the finished television. Sub-assembly may take place in one country, with final assembly of the whole television taking place in another.

Unless all the businesses involved work to the same standard, the parts will not be able to be assembled properly. This working together is known as interdependence.

Standards in Real Life

To illustrate how important quality standards are, consider this case study on MC Fire Protection Ltd.

MC Fire Protection was established by Mike Chilman and is based in Bicester, Oxfordshire. It has been providing fire protection services for over 30 years. The company employs a team responsible for covering the supply, installation and maintenance of fire extinguishers and fire alarm systems.

It also offers a consultancy service for all aspects of fire risk management. The company has earned an impressive reputation in the fire industry.

Changes in British and European legislation and demands from insurance companies are causing an increase in sales of fire systems. Businesses are legally required to take steps to protect themselves, staff and customers from the danger of fire.

Fire protection relies heavily on fire extinguishers and fire alarms. These have to comply with the fire safety standards. This means that users are confident the equipment will do its job.

Companies that provide fire risk assessments and consultancy services use these industry standards. By obtaining ISO 9001 registration, the company can show that the whole service is professional and quality assured.

The Managing Director of MC Fire Protection, Mike Chilman, explains why ISO registration is so important.

> *'In 2004 our competitors were starting to publicise the fact that they complied with ISO 9001. Many businesses prefer to trade with companies that comply with recognised standards rather than with those that do not. On a practical level, ISO 9001 had made positive changes with improvements to our workshop, supply chain and record-keeping.*
>
> *'All the standards we apply have brought us extra reassurance. They help to show we are more professional, while our customers are confident that the services we provide are high quality. I would recommend standards to other businesses in the fire protection industry – in fact, it's becoming more and more of a necessity.'*

Today we live in a complex global economy. Relationships are frequently built on reputations for supplying quality products, services and processes. BSI plays a key role in creating the standards and in testing.

As international trade, travel and communications increase, international standards are used to enable products to be traded across Europe and worldwide. BSI is actively involved in helping UK and other international businesses to build their own reputations for quality through standards.

SUSTAINABLE BUSINESS AT CORUS

Steel is 100% recyclable and can be used time and time again with no loss of quality.

Corus is the UK's biggest steel manufacturer and employs nearly 50,000 people in 40 countries. It is the eighth largest steel maker in the world with an annual turnover of nearly £10 billion. Corus has major steelworks in the UK at various locations including Port Talbot, Scunthorpe, Teesside and Rotherham.

Steel making is a very competitive business. In 2004, Corus launched a programme called 'Restoring Success', which aims to give the company a lead over rivals in efficient production.

This programme focuses on eliminating wasteful activities and ensuring efficient production. A key part of this is an emphasis on recycling steel. Through its strong recycling credentials, Corus stands out from its rivals as a responsible business that is committed to sustainable development.

The world economy is growing at a staggering rate. New economies in India and China, each with more than a billion people, have joined the global trading system.

This means that the demand for resources such as metal has grown significantly. Steel is a metal that lies at the heart of our industrial system, providing the structure and raw material for a vast range of products.

Steel possesses one specific quality that makes it superior to many other metals -it is 100% recyclable and can be used time and time again with no loss of quality.

WHAT IS SUSTAINABLE DEVELOPMENT?

The World Commission on Environment in 1987 stated that 'sustainable development meets the needs of the present without compromising the ability of future generations to meet their own needs'. This definition contains three basic ideas:

Sustainability is everyone's responsibility:

- Individuals must act in a sustainable way. We should aim to reduce our carbon footprint and support the environment, for example, by not wasting energy or making unnecessary journeys.
- Governments must work together to set targets and limits on environmental pollution.
- Businesses such as Corus must behave in a sustainable way.

THE CHALLENGES OF SUSTAINABLE DEVELOPMENT

The challenges facing Corus include, among others, waste management, energy conservation, risk management and recycling. Corus tackles these through an integrated approach to environmental management.

Corus'

Corus invests heavily in research and development to create better products for its customers and for society as a whole activities are focused on steel. Its products are durable, adaptable, reusable and recyclable. It is therefore possible to create ways of managing negative impacts on the environment.

For example:

- Corus makes sure that all wastes are handled properly. It has created key targets for managing and reducing emissions.

- Corus continually seeks new ways of reducing the amount of energy used in its manufacturing and recycling operations.
- A high priority is given to risk management to reduce the number of accidents at work.

Corus' products are essential to modern life. For example, Corus steel is used in affordable packaging and energy-efficient modular homes and buildings like the new Olympic stadium, as well as in lighter, stronger and safer transport systems, such as trams.

Why Sustainability is Important

Corus is the largest steel recycler in the UK. Corus Steel Packaging Recycling promotes the recovery of used steel packaging to:

- consumers
- local authorities, waste management companies and collectors
- businesses and its customers.

Steel is unrivalled as a sustainable packaging material for a number of reasons:

- Steel is derived from two of the earth's most plentiful natural resources – iron ore and limestone.
- Steel can be recycled time and time again without any loss of quality.
- Steel is easy to extract from the waste stream using kerbside collections, can banks
- and magnetic extraction.
- Steel scrap will be recycled and re-used to make new steel products.

Environmental Benefits

Recycling steel has major environmental benefits. By recycling steel, Corus can:

- help preserve natural resources
- help protect the environment
- meet government targets for reducing waste – the longer-term target for recycling steel packaging is 55% by 2010.

Steel is the most recycled packaging material in Europe. All steel packaging is 100% recyclable. European steel currently contains at least 54% recycled steel.

Levels of Recycling

Corus is working hard to make the public aware that all steel packaging can and should be recycled. Research undertaken by Corus in partnership with ASDA in 2005 demonstrated this point.

The people questioned showed a relatively high knowledge about what steel packaging products could be recycled. However, when questioned about which of these products they actively recycled, the results were:

It is clear that there is still work to be done to increase consumer awareness of the wide range of steel packaging that can be recycled.

Corus wants to make the public aware how steel packaging can be re-used through a closed loop 'steel to steel' recycling process. Consumers play a key part in this continuous loop process.

If they recycle the steel products they buy in the first part of the loop, these enter the production chain in the second part.

So the steel travels from the consumer, to the recycling box, then to the recycling facility.

The steel is then transformed at the steel reprocessor and shipped back to manufacturers ready for re-use as new products. This creates a continual cycle of steel re-use which can happen many times.

Sustainability and Stakeholders

One of the most important choices a company makes is how to use its scarce resources. Corus seeks to balance the needs of its stakeholders by building sustainable development principles into all aspects of business activity.

The 'steel cycle'

The 'steel cycle' shows how four main stakeholder groups are involved in steel recycling:

1. consumers
2. manufacturers of steel products (such as Corus)
3. supermarkets that sell steel packaging to us and provide recycling banks
4. local authorities that provide local recycling facilities.

Wider Involvement

Corus is involved in wider industry and international steel groups such as the International Iron and Steel Institute (IISI).

This group promotes sustainable steel manufacturing on a global scale and supports recycling initiatives.

On the IISI website an interesting film clip, 'Steel and You' demonstrates the various ways in which steel plays a part in our lives, as well as the importance of recycling and responsible steel manufacture.

In addition, Corus has its own education programme.

This includes a new website called SCRIB where people can download educational and fun activities in English and Welsh to increase their recycling knowledge.

Benefits and Costs of Recycling

A benefit is anything that has a positive impact. It can be internal to the business or affect individuals and groups outside the business. A cost is anything that has a negative impact. It can be either internal or external.

When examining benefits and costs, it is standard practice to try to measure them.

The usual way to do this is to attach a monetary value to the costs and benefits.

Businesses carry out decisions when the benefits outweigh the costs.

By continually monitoring its performance, Corus is increasingly able to reduce costs and deliver benefits to stakeholders.

Corus enjoys both social and financial benefits from recycling. Everyone can see how the company is actively working to improve the environment. A cost-benefit analysis has also shown that the benefits of recycling are much greater than the costs.

Key Performance Indicators

The performance of a company can be measured by creating Key Performance Indicators (KPIs). These give the company targets to work towards and help to measure success.

Corus has created a number of KPIs that focus on becoming more sustainable including:

- by 2010, reducing total energy consumption in the UK by 11.5% compared to 1997
- by 2010, increasing the steel packaging recycling rate in the UK to 55%
- achieving compliance with required emission levels.

CONCLUSION

We are all stakeholders in how well steel is used and recycled.

Corus creates policies and operates plans to use steel in a sustainable way. Government and supermarkets are working together to create the recycling facilities but we as consumers play a vital role in the steel cycle.

The steel packaging we put in can banks or kerbside recycling boxes are recycled over and over again without any loss of quality. If we behave in a responsible way with this, we can make an important contribution to sustainability.

6

Contract and Cost Management

The purpose of IGLC championship white papers is to explain the area of inquiry and to invite researchers and practitioners to collaborate and to contribute papers. Our first task is to define the championship.

DEFINITION OF THE CHAMPIONSHIP AREA

The theme of Contract and Cost Management covers the legal and financial infrastructure which underpins the design, construction and operation of buildings and structures and an be aligned to the primary functions of the production management model. Central to this theme is the investigation of the relationship between risk and reward across the project and the search for radically new lean definitions and methods of allocation and management.

Construction is widely accepted as a high risk industry subject to much uncertainty and variation with production systems redesigned to some degree for each project phase (definition, design, assembly, commissioning), and to a lesser degree, redesigned every day. Variability in the composition of the project team, client requirement and design solution challenge management activities at all levels and the constellation of interdependent tasks that change daily give rise to dynamic problem solving activities embedded deep within the processes. At their best, these activities form an agile, responsive project delivery process, at their worst they cause immeasurable damage to the project success as a result of wide spread action without co-ordination, integration or collaboration.

The challenge is to maintain the problem solving abilities but prevent unilateral action within a satisfactory economic framework. This framework includes and derives from the procurement systems which initiate and govern the design, construction and operation of a structure or facility. Procurement systems set up the relationships between parties enshrining within a contract/s the scope of work, the allocation of obligation and risk and the mechanisms for agreeing costs. The parties to a project span from the Client through consultants and contractors across to trade crews, suppliers and manufacturers. All are involved at various points in the design, delivery and operation of the structure or facility. In an industry where most cases of dispute result from unfulfilled expectations and many of the management activities focus on the symptoms rather than the root cause of the problems suggests the focus on risk has tended to overlook the primary risk that value not be delivered to the client within client-specified constraints, and that the best way to manage that risk is to assure project success.

There are three aspects to the investigation of this theme:

1. The first task is to design the contractual structure of the project and to establish its objectives and constraints (relational contracting, setting target values and costs) in. the pursuit of value generation and waste elimination.
2. The second task is to manage project execution toward those objectives and within those constraints (project governance; designing to target values and costs)and

3. The third task is to learn from breakdowns (unintended deviations from standard/plan) and from experiments (intended deviations from standard/ plan).

The three aspects are of course interrelated and require the critical evaluation of the purposes, products and processes of contract and cost management. The fundamental issue being if and how the management of projects should and can change in response to new thinking in the management of production (designing and making) on those projects. For example, is it feasible and optimal to continue to procure, contract, evaluate and pay in traditional ways on projects implementing lean project delivery?

THE RESEARCH AGENDA

Construction cost control has been based on the thermostat model; i.e., budgets allocate money to cost accounts and spending is tracked to detect negative variances from budget, which triggers corrective action.

This approach parallels the generation of detailed activity schedules at the beginning of projects, which allocate time to activities. Unfortunately, the only thing we know for sure about a detailed schedule or budget at the beginning of a project is that the project will not be completed according to that schedule or budget.

The level of detail must be matched to the degree of uncertainty so we don't confuse speculation and desire with a real plan. The allocation of both time and money to activities must be done in progressively greater detail through the course of a project. And rather than concentrating effort on tracking actual spending against those allocations, we need time and cost management systems that help project teams make good decisions regarding time and cost.

This approach is being applied at the Boldt Companies; a construction contractor based in Appleton, Wisconsin. Cost reports are simplified and cost control is distributed to various levels in the company, following a philosophy of distributed decision making rather than central command. The goal is to have real time information on project cost and schedule status, and to continuously scan for risks and opportunities, producing for clients no less often than monthly, a set of alternative action plans for completing the project successfully, while maximizing customer value.

It is clear that collaboration underpins all Lean Construction activity. It is equally clear that the primary barrier to collaboration is the ability of companies to maintain their economic integrity.

This applies equally to all project participants be they Clients, contractors, trade crews, manufacturers, consultants etc. Each party desires to reduce their risk exposure and protect themselves against variation and uncertainty by including contingency (time, money and materials). Where we talk about "lowering the water in the river" to stress the system and reveal constraints in project delivery, contingency forms a major part of the "water" upon which the project floats.

The Last Planner System delivers time compression and goes some way towards JIT in reducing materials contingency but money buffers have yet to be fully addressed. How to remove contingency and maintain economic integrity is challenging – open book cost reimbursement contracts can move towards this helping money flow across organisational boundaries in search of the best project-level investment opportunity..

So there is a need to be creative in incentivising performance and negotiating targets for delivering best value that fairly rewards risk management for all parties and this needs to be a design requirement for contractual structures. Perhaps the crucial item here is defining best value. This certainly is not least cost although many construction projects are let, managed and judged on their cost performance.

Questions arising from these issues include:-

1. How can value be redefined in order to shift the focus from least-cost based judgements.
2. How can the differing values across the project delivery process and/or for differing project parties be defined and reconciled?
3. Would the evaluation of benefits or outcomes provide a new way of thinking about value?
4. How can contingency (money) become more visible and then be compressed?
5. Cash flow is essential for business. How can the activity of making payments across the supply chain be improved? Can we develop radically new methods for making cash flow?
6. Budgets & targets are an important part of the investment decision for Clients. They are also critical for bidding strategy and business case decisions for the supply chain. How can we radically change our thinking about defining these?
7. The Theory of Constraints (Goldrat) showed us that utilisation was not a good measure of profitability and throughput was more meaningful. Are we similarly measuring the wrong things and believing projects to be profitable erroneously?
8. Lean accounting is a simplification of accounting processes with much less emphasis on traditional labour, plant, material and overhead costing. What can be learned from this for construction accounting?

9. New methods of contracting that require collaboration and integration across the supply chain demand different behaviour from the parties. What sort of behaviour will be required and can behaviour be related to the contract clauses (e.g., see IGLC and LCI papers on relational contracting)?
10. How can trust be developed across the supply chain ensuring fair payment within a transparent economic framework?
11. Stability is a precursor to change and innovation, how can we move construction towards economic stability and level demand?

The above points are by no means exhaustive and it is expected that these areas will be refined and new areas will emerge as the theme of Contract and Cost Management develops in the coming years.

Your comments and suggestions for improving and expanding the above are warmly requested. Our task as a learning community is to dig into the details, evaluate experiments, and push our knowledge beyond its current boundaries.

There is no Indian policy document which examines waste as part of a cycle of production-consumption-recovery or perceives waste through a prism of overall sustainability. In fact, interventions have been fragmented and are often contradictory. The new Municipal Solid Waste Management Rules 2000, which came into effect from January 2004, fail even to manage waste in a cyclic process. Waste management still is a linear system of collection and disposal, creating health and environmental hazards.

Urban India is likely to face a massive waste disposal problem in the coming years. Until now, the problem of waste has been seen as one of cleaning and disposing as rubbish. But a closer look at the current and future scenario reveals that waste needs to be treated holistically, recognising its natural resource roots as well as health impacts. Waste can be wealth, which has tremendous potential not only for generating livelihoods for the urban poor but can also enrich the earth through composting and recycling rather than spreading pollution as has been the case. Increasing urban migration and a high density of population will make waste management a difficult issue to handle in the near future, if a new paradigm for approaching it is not created.

Developing countries such as India are undergoing a massive migration of their population from rural to urban centres. New consumption patterns and social linkages are emerging. India will have more than 40 per cent, i.e. over 400 million people, clustered in cities over the next thirty years (UN, 1995). Modern urban living brings on the problem of waste, which increases in quantity, and changes in composition with each passing day. There is, however, an inadequate understanding of the problem, both of infrastructure requirements as well as its social dimensions. Urban planners, municipal agencies, environmental regulators, labour groups, citizens' groups and non-governmental organisations need to develop a variety of responses which are rooted in local dynamics, rather than borrow non-contextual solutions from elsewhere.

There have been a variety of policy responses to the problem of urban solid waste in India, especially over the past few years, yet sustainable solutions either of organic or inorganic waste remain untapped and unattended. All policy documents as well as legislation dealing with urban solid waste mention or acknowledge recycling as one of the ways of diverting waste, but they do so in a piece-meal manner and do not address the framework needed to enable this to happen. Critical issues such as industry responsibility, a critical paradigm to enable sustainable recycling and to catalyse waste reduction through, say better packing, have not been touched upon.

Any new paradigm should include a cradle-to-grave approach with responsibility being shared by many stakeholders, including product manufacturers, consumers and communities, the recycling industry, trade, municipalities and the urban poor.

WHAT IS OUR WASTE?

Consumption, linked to per capita income, has a strong relationship with waste generation. As per capita income rises, more savings are spent on goods and services, especially when the transition is from a low income to a middle-income level. Urbanisation not only concentrates waste, but also raises generation rates since rural consumers consume less than urban ones. India will probably see a rise in waste generation from less than 40,000 metric tonnes per year to over 125,000 metric tonnes by the year 2030 (Srishti, 2000). Technologies, which can process organic wastes have to be a mainstay to any solution. The Supreme Court appointed the Burman Committee (1999), which rightly recommended that composting should be carried out in each municipality. Composting is probably the easiest and most appropriate technology to deal with a majority of our waste, given its organic nature.

However, new and expensive technologies are being pushed to deal with our urban waste problem, ignoring their environmental and social implications. It is particularly true in the case of thermal treatment of waste using technologies such as gasification, incineration, pyrolysis or pellatisation. Indian waste content does not provide enough fuel value (caloric value) for profitable energy production (and is unlikely to do so soon). It needs the addition of auxiliary fuel or energy. Such technologies put communities to risk and are opposed widely. For example, the United States has not been able to install a new incinerator for the past five years, while costs for burning garbage have escalated astronomically with rising environmental standards in Europe.

For developing countries, recycling of waste is the most economically viable option available both in terms of employment generation for the urban poor with no skills and investment.

Pyrolysis - Risky, but Favoured

While the more developed countries are doing away with incinerators because of high costs (due to higher standards of emission control), developing countries have become potential markets for dumping such technologies. Incinerators routinely emit dioxins, furans and polychlorinated by-phenyls (PCB), which are deadly toxins, casing cancer and endocrine system damage.

Other conventional toxins such as mercury, heavy metals are also released. Pollution control costs for incinerators can exceed over 50 per cent of their already astronomical cost, and an incinerator for 2,000 metric tonnes of waste per day can cost over 500 million US dollars. Ironically, the better the air control works, the more pollutants are transferred to land and water, through scrubbers and filters and the problem of safe landfill disposal of the ash remains.

Again, such measures go against the requirements of the Municipal Solid Waste Management Rules 2000, which asks for source segregation of waste for cleaner composting and recycling. The lessons of incinerating Indian urban waste do not seem to have been learnt, despite a disastrous experience with a Dutch-funded incinerator in Delhi. It ran for just one week in 1984, since the calorific value of the fuel was less than half of that the incinerator needed.

Policy Responses

At the national policy level, the ministry of environment and forests has recently legislated the Municipal Waste Management and Handling Rules 2000. This law details the practices to be followed by the various municipalities for managing urban waste. However, the response has been segmented and far from satisfactory.

First, it does not address mechanisms which will be needed for promoting recycling, or waste minimisation. Secondly, there is no provision for any public participation, despite the fact that the Rules have been an outcome of public pressure and the immense work done by non-government organisations and community groups in this area.

Other recent policy documents include the Ministry of Urban Affairs' Shukla Committee's Report (January 2000) the Supreme Court appointed Burman Committee's Report (March 1999), and the Report of the National Plastic Waste Management Task Force (August 1997).

But the present rules and regulations are inadequate both in terms of assessing environmental impact of waste and its economic and social implications.

For developing countries, recycling of waste is the most economically viable option available both in terms of employment generation for the urban poor with no skills and investment.

Indirectly this also preserves the natural resources going down the drains. Some local governments have taken initiatives to burn waste through incineration or gasification for insignificant electricity generation at astronomical cost and with dangerous environmental impacts, and which will take away the livelihoods of hundreds of thousands of the urban poor.

URBAN POVERTY, INFORMAL RECYCLING SECTOR AND LIVELIHOOD QUESTIONS

Urban poverty is inextricably linked with waste. In India alone, over a million people find livelihood opportunities in the area of waste; they are engaged in waste collection (popularly known as ragpicking) and recycling through well-organised systems. A substantial population of urban poor in other developing countries also earn their livelihood through waste. It is important to understand issues of waste in this context. The informal sector dealing with waste is engaged in various types of work like waste picking, sorting, recycling and at the organised level, door-to-door collection, composting and recycling recovery. The municipalities in many developing countries do not do any recycling recovery on their own.

Recycling of only some types of materials like plastics, paper and metals is not enough. A recycling research carried out by Srishti revealed that many types of new materials mainly used for packaging are not, or indeed cannot be, recycled in the low-end technology being employed.

Besides, there are serious issues of poor occupational safety provisions of the waste pickers as well as workers. This sector faces a severe threat from the new business model approach to managing waste being promoted, without any attempts to integrate existing systems in them. There is an urgent need to build upon existing systems instead of attempting to replace them blindly with models from developed countries.

The Ministry of Urban Development and Poverty Alleviation, as well as Agriculture, should develop the market for compost, and if required provide subsidies for compost manure – first to provide organic soil nutrients to the farmers and to solve the urban waste problem which continuously is polluting land through uncontrolled dumping.

India's Green Revolution rescued the nation from famines, but left over 11.6 million hectares of low-productivity, nutrient-depleted soils ruined by unbalanced and excessive use of synthetic fertilisers and lack of organic manure or micronutrients.

City compost can fill this need and solve both the problems of barren land and organic nutrient shortages, estimated at six million tons a year.

India's 35 largest cities alone can provide 5.7 million tonnes a year of organic manure if their biodegradable waste is composted and returned to the soil. Integrated plant nutrient management, using city compost along with synthetic fertilisers, can generate enormous national savings as well as cleaning urban India. There is scarcely any other national programme which can bring such huge benefits to both urban and rural sectors.

Municipal Response

The Green Revolution left over 11.6 million hectares of low-productivity, nutrient-depleted soils ruined by unbalanced and excessive use of synthetic fertilisers and lack of organic manure or micronutrients. City compost can fill this need and solve both the problems of barren land and organic nutrient shortages.

- Treating garbage right
- No wasteful business this!

At another level, the trend in cities in developing countries is to shift the traditional municipal responsibility to private actors without considering the host of existing stakeholders. Also upstream focuses such as making producers responsible for packaging waste are lacking. Excessive reliance is placed on technologies many of which are expensive with high environmental and economic ramifications. For instance, installing an incinerator leaves the question of waste recycling - or toxic environmental impacts - unanswered.

Merely replacing one centralised system by another does not change waste behaviour on its own, or ensure continued livelihood opportunities for those who live off waste such as waste-pickers. It also does not ensure that economically deprived communities in metropolitan cities in particular (four metropolitan cities have nearly more then 300,000 livelihoods) and 40 per cent of the urban poor have cleaner neighbourhoods. Often such replacement has direct and hidden subsidies, mostly at the expense of poorer communities and the environment. For instance, waste disposal sifting is often done in poorer neighbourhoods, leading to groundwater and other types of contamination.

Though community projects are working well and fulfilling the greater objectives of environmental safety and natural resource conservation, they are doing so under great economic and social stress. There is neither the recognition nor support for such work by the different institutions from various stakeholders. Hence there is a need to bring the work into the larger public space and review the rules and regulations both for enhancing and providing incentive to such community waste management systems.

Composting: the Environmentally and Economically Sustainable Solution

Composting of city wastes is a legal requirement provided under the Municipal Solid Waste Management (MSW) Rules 2000 for all municipal bodies in the country. But neither the central nor the state governments have yet responded to show any kind of preparedness for it, nor have they been able to grasp it as an environmental and social good that requires official support which can generate employment. The MSW Rules 2000 requires that "biodegradable wastes shall be processed by composting, vermi-composting, anaerobic digestion or any other appropriate biological processing for the stabilisation of wastes". The specified deadline for setting up of waste processing and disposal facilities was 31 December 2003 or earlier.

The production and sale of city compost is not the primary function of city administrations, but it will need to be privatised for optimum efficiency and care. Several entrepreneurs have already entered the field and many compost plants are in place, almost all on public land made available at a nominal cost. These companies are willing to wait for the five to seven years payback on their investment, but are facing tremendous problems of producing compost from unsegregated wastes, and of marketing and distributing their product. The government is indifferent to the problems of these compost producers (i.e. a working capital crunch because of highly seasonal demand) and to farmers' needs (i.e., timely, easily accessible availability of affordable compost).

The Fertiliser Association of India, the leading lobby group for synthetic fertilisers, is focused on protecting the fertiliser producers' massive subsidies (Rs 142,500 million annually) for their chemical fertilisers – subsidies from which the farmers do not benefit. This situation is increasingly coming under national debate. Just 12 per cent of this annual subsidy would meet the one-time capital cost of city compost plants in India's 400 largest cities (which include cities with populations of over 100,000 people) and would be able to produce 5.7 million tonnes a year of organic soil conditioners. Integrated plant nutrient management (IPNM) would also reduce the foreign exchange burden on the Indian exchequer because bulk supplies of phosphorus and potassium must be imported. In addition, the government of India spends Rs 43.19 million on phosphorus and potassium concessions alone. (Phosphorous is used to store and transfer energy within the plant. It is used in forming nucleic acids (DNA, RNA). Potassium remains in tissues in ionic form and is not used in the synthesis of new compounds as are nitrogen and phosphorous. Potassium is mobile in plants and tends to move from older to younger, more active growing tissue.)

Emphasising IPNM using city compost, which can be produced all over the country can be a successful strategy if a focused inter-ministerial effort is made. However, in spite of the fact that the Ministry of Agriculture renamed its Department of Fertilisers as the "Department of Integrated Nutrient Management" a year ago, no policy changes have taken place whatsoever. A proposed Task Force including the agriculture and fertiliser ministries may soon formulate an Action Plan for IPNM.

The real economic benefits of compost use, like improved soil quality, water retention, biological activity, micronutrient content and improved pest resistance of crops, are ignored by policy-makers and fertiliser producers. Fertiliser producers do not yet realise that preventing soil depletion and reclaiming degraded soils would in fact increase the size of the market and therefore, also their market share, which is currently threatened by globalisation and world prices that undercut their own. Since most large fertiliser plants are government-owned, another threat is the government's intended policy of closing down loss-making public-sector enterprises and disinvesting from profitable ones.

Preliminary surveys on municipalities' preparedness in implementing the MSW Rules 2000 show that the majority of the cities are yet to embark on city-wide implementation of door-to-door collection of waste, source segregation, composting of organics, recycling and creating engineered and safe landfill sites for residual waste disposal. The municipalities were given three years time to make such preparations but most of them have not even woken up. This is the regard given to the apex court's verdict. Whether municipalities will enforce the MSW Rules 2000 and provide cleaner and healthier cities is yet to be seen. For now, the risk remains that MSW Rules will become yet another policy to gather dust due to government apathy.

7

Strategic Cost Management

Strategic Cost Management (SCM) has been a powerful management tool for the last decade. In this paper an attempt has been made to explain the reforms initiated in the power sector at the centre and the states using the various approaches used in SCM. The paper illustrates the role of SCM in this volatile industry confronted with evolving regulation and stiffening competition, and also in dealing with the problems of on-going reforms.

INTRODUCTION

The conventional cost management is based on the assumption that the cost can be controlled or reduced or managed by changing volume, improving labour productivity, or reducing overheads. Its focus is inward, emphasizing the process of cost control and cost reduction, oblivious of the other opportunities. Therefore, conventional cost management, it is said,“ starts too late and ends too early” and in the process ignores linkages and the process of value creation outside the firm’s boundariesi. SCM addresses this limitation and expands the cost management beyond the firm’s boundaries. SCM blends three important strategic analytic approaches viz. value chain analysis, strategic positioning analysis and cost driver analysis, taken from the strategic management literatureii:

Value chain analysis basically focuses on value creation by identifying value activities such as, firm infrastructure, procurement, technology, human-resource management, in-bound logistics, operations, out-bound logistics, sales and services and seeks to establish linkages among these activities to achieve optimal efficiency in terms of cost and benefit. In a larger sense this approach can be extended beyond the firm so as to include the suppliers' value chain, channels value chain and customers' value chain.

Strategic positioning analysis basically emphasizes that instead of competing in the same product-market if a company could choose a product market scope not covered by others, the chances of success would be better. Such positioning would be in terms of cost leadership,

Dr. Ramana is an Associate Professor (Accounting and Finance Area), Xavier Institute of Management, Bhubaneswar-751013.

SCM focusing on certain target segment, or producing a distinct product not produced by others. Strategic positioning can also be conceptualized in terms of product portfolio positioning inside the company using the concept of product life cycle.

Cost drivers analysis, basically seeks to identify all factors affecting the cost. In conventional cost management, cost are collected on the basis of the centers or departments and allocated to products using the process of primary and secondary allocation using approximate bases, which in many cases result in distortions in cost estimates and consequently to inaccurate pricing and other managerial decisions. Cost driver analysis seeks to eliminate such distortions.

Each of these approaches is explained and illustrated using the power sector scenario.

SCM Perspective

Lack of commercial orientation, unrealistic pricing policies and variety of other factors had led many state electricity boards into sickness. The aggregate losses of SEBs more than quadrupled in the last decade. In fact, four of the eighteen major SEBs incurred a loss of Rs.1000 crore each in 99-00.

Some of the reasons for such disastrous performance of SEBs are the increasing gap between the tariff and cost, sub-optimal capital structure, low plant load factor (PLF), high transmission and distribution (T&D) losses, insufficient capital expenditure, and inability of the state governments to support the sector. This prompted the Government of India to initiate reforms with the following objectives:

- to break up the monolithic structure of the SEBs into more manageable and viable distribution zones;
- to create a regulatory mechanism which could set down the technical and financial parameters for performance, the guidelines for tariff setting, and also function as a moderator to balance the interests of all stakeholders;
- to encourage greater participation by privately owned enterprises in the activities of electricity generation, supply and distribution.

In this paper, the first component of the reforms i.e. breaking the monolithic structures of SEB has been explained using SCM.

As mentioned above, one of the major themes of SCM is the Value Chain Analysis (VCA). The value chain for any firm in any business is the linked set of value-creating activities all the way from basic raw material sources to the ultimate end-use product delivered into the final SCM consumers' handsiii. VCA has been widely used as a means of describing the activities within and around an organisation, and relating them to an assessment of the competitive strength of an organisation. One of the key aspects of VCA is the recognition that organisations are much more than a random collection of machines, money, and people. Moreover, these resources are of no value unless deployed into activities and organised into routines and systems, which ensure that products/services are produced which are valued by the final consumerv.

In order to understand the inherent strengths of business one has to identify the value activities within and outside the organisation. While Porter focused on the value creating activities within an organisation, under the concept of SCM, Shank and Govindrajanvi extended the concept and argued that a firm's value chain is embedded in a larger system that includes suppliers' and customers' value chains.

VCA emphasises that a firm should adopt one of the following strategies to survive and then excel in the industry:

- manage the cost drivers better than the competitors, or
- Change the position on the value chain

The un-bundling of SEBs, as we will see in the following paragraphs, is being attempted with the above objectives.

Pre-Reforms: Vertically Integrated Organisation-OSEB covering the entire Value Chain

SEBs are vertically integrated organisation having under its control all aspects of electricity business: from generation to supply of power to the ultimate consumer. Value chain of vertically integrated SEBs covering all the aspects of the industry is shown below:

- Generation
- Transmission

- Distribution
- OSEB

Since SEBs' operations are spread over the entire value chain, they were not able to perform satisfactorily in any activity. Some of major negative performance indicators of SEBs are:

SCM:

- Overall availability of power: Lack of resources and delays in project implementation have led to insufficient generating-capacity growth, resulting in serious shortages of supply vis-à-vis demand.
- Generation: Low plant load factor (PLF): India's PLF is 64.7%
- Transmission and Distribution: T&D losses are over 40% far higher than the international standard. High losses can be attributed to obsolete distribution network, and theft of power in different forms. In some states, the T&D losses are more than 50%. In many SEB the total collection is around 70-80% of the total billing.
- Financial Performance of the sector: The total state subsidies amounted to at least Rs.143 billion (in 1998-99). Even with these subsidies SEB losses amounted to above Rs. 20 billion.

Prior to the reforms, OSEB' s operations also covered the entire value chain. The Table-I speaks volumes about the performance of OSEB and some of the SEBs and raises doubts about its very survival.

First Phase of Reforms: Formation of new organisations for different Value Activities

In the first phase of the reforms it was realised that an organisation cannot operate efficiently in all the activities if it tries to capture the entire value chain. The realisation that these are separate activities with separate cost drivers led to the first phase reforms in Orissa, AP, Rajasthan, and Haryana. Accordingly, in Orissa the erstwhile OSEB was unbundled as follows:

- The thermal generation plants were transferred to Orissa Power Generation Corporation (OPGC)
- The hydel generation plants were transferred to a new created Orissa Hydro Power Corporation (OHPC)
- Transmission and Distribution business was transferred to Grid Corporation of Orissa Ltd (Gridco).

For the purpose of this paper we will focus our attention of the Transmission and Distribution business i.e. Gridco. However, while analysing the comparative position of Gridco effort will be made to cover the entire value chain. Important activities of Gridco are acquiring power from the generating stations, maintaining the transmission lines (Transmission) and selling the same to the distribution companies.

One of the limitations of the above presentation is that the information provided will not of much use for the various managerial decisions and even it fails in explaining the very nature of business. Some of the important managerial issues that cannot be answered by the above statement are as follows:

- What is the composition of revenue?
- Is it possible to reduce the cost of power?
- What percentage of the expenditure is for the transmission or distribution of power?
- What is the allocation of assets for different activities and consequently the respective share of depreciation and interest?

In order to get answers for the above issues it may be useful to organise the above information in the value chain framework. On the basis of the above table it is difficult to say which business is profitable. Since both businesses are under one management, unless there is inter-unit transfer price from transmission to distribution business it may not be possible to determine the profit of each activity. But how to determine the price of the power transferred by the transmission division to the distribution division? The price can be determined on the basis of the recovery of the cost/ market price/price approved by the regulator. For the purpose of the analysis let us assume that the power has been transferred at no-profit-no-loss basis, though the regulator may not allow all expenses as pass-through. In the above situation, the entire loss may be attributed to the distribution business.

Above table demonstrates the usefulness of presenting the financial data of Gridco using the VCA framework. It shows that the transmission and distribution business require different managerial skill. The transmission business requires the technical expertise whereas the distribution business requires more of the commercial skills. Any decision to restructure Gridco should recognise the existence of two different business activities.

Further Division of Value Chain

Since the cost drivers of the transmission and distribution business are different and requires different business strategies, it was decided to put the businesses under different management. The distribution business of Gridco was transferred to four newly formed companies viz. s was transferred to WESCO, NESCO, Southco, and CESCO (Distribution companies) and later on the distribution companies were privatised.

With such a transfer, Gridco is able to focus it managerial attention on a particular part of the industry's value chain i.e. transmission business. Gridco's main activities are to buy power from the generating companies, maintain the transmission system, and sell and wheel the power to four distribution companies and other states.

In the post reform period, seven firms operate in the value chain, wherein each firm focuses its resources on a particular segment of the value chain.

Gridco acquires power from the generating companies at a price negotiated and accepted as per the power purchase agreements (PPA) and sell the same to the distribution companies and other states at a price approved by the regulator (OERC).

The above presentation on the basis of the VCA provides interesting insights of the power sector. Though the cost of input for both Transmission and Distribution business is around 82%, the cost of running the business i.e. Transmission cost and Distribution cost is 14 % and 251% respectively.

It clearly demonstrates that major business risk is in the distribution activity. Moreover, the distribution business also has the problems of revenue management because of the large number of customers spread over a wide geographical area. The large customer base consisting of different categories ranging from small domestic user to a large industrial user further complicates the business.

The above presentation also shows the relationship between the various players in a value chain. For instance, Gridco's performance depends on the performance of the suppliers and its customers. In order to make the sector vibrant and commercially viable, it is necessary that each component of the value chain should operate efficiently. The sector cannot survive by having small pockets of prosperity, which is the case at present. At present the generating companies are making profits, and the transmission company can easily break-even in the near future. However, to make the sector vibrant and efficient it is necessary to address the problems of the distribution business too.

In fact distribution is the weakest link on the value chain. It is necessary that the all forms of reforms should take place in the distribution side of the value chain.

Cost Drivers of different Value Activities

In the conventional cost management, volume is considered to be the most important driver of the costix. SCM, on the other hand recognises the fact that the cost is caused and driven by many factors that are interrelated too. The conventional cost management uses GAAP based accounting data for various decisions.

Such dependence on accounting distorts the cost data and affects the decisions based on such data. Therefore, Porter has said 'while accounting systems do contain useful data for cost analysis, they often get in the way of strategic cost analysis.' Porterx identified some important cost drivers and stressed that volume is not the only cost driver. Similarly Shank and Govindrajan classified the cost drivers into structural and executional cost driversxi.

As mentioned in one of the above paragraphs, since the cost drivers of the different parts of the value chain of the power sector are different, it really makes sense to unbundle the SEBs into generation, transmission, and distribution.

In the transmission business one can manage the operations only by understanding the following drivers of the cost:

a) Composition of power purchase, not just the quantity: For transmission business viz. Gridco, it is important to control the cost of power purchased. The Cost per unit is Rs. 1.14. However, the driver is not the quantity alone. In order to manage the cost and in the process reduce it may be necessary for Gridco to understand its composition. Gridco acquires power from more than eight sources. The cost differs from source to source depending on the PPA.

It is evident from the above table that Gridco has to spend time on understanding the composition and determine the optimum combination of the sources. The cost per unit of power purchased varies in the range of 45 paise to 235 paise. Moreover, the Gridco should also understand the cost drivers of some of the suppliers. For instance power acquired from OPGC accounts for 27% of total revenue of Gridco. Such analysis of the suppliers' cost drivers will be necessary in the future when the distribution companies will be allowed to acquire power from the generators directly.

b) Proper maintenance of transmission lines: The technical losses i.e. the difference between units purchased and units sold can be reduced only by proper maintenance of the transmission lines. The regulator has also instructed Gridco to take steps for reducing this loss.

c) Proper control of the capital expenditure: We have seen in one of the previous paragraphs, that the transmission business is a capital intensive one. Controlling capital expenditure is an important managerial issue for Gridco as it affects the depreciation, interest and consequently the allowable tariff.

Whereas, in the case of the distribution business one requires to pay attention to the following drivers of the cost and consequently the business:

a) Managing the revenue cycle: For a distribution business managing the revenue cycle is of utmost importance. It consists of meter reading, billing, and cash collection. Each of these activities requires special attention of the management.

b) Control of the non-technical losses: One of the consequences of the bad management of the revenue cycle is the increasing gap between the power purchased and power sold. This difference may be due to power theft at all levels of revenue cycle.

c) Composition of customers: Consumers of a distribution company can be divided into two broad categories viz. domestic and industrial consumers. Power is supplied at high voltage to the industrial customers, whereas it is supplied at a lower voltage to the domestic consumers.

The differences in the cost and business drivers require a different style and strategy of management. One can say that Gridco's decision to concentrate on a particular part of the value chain and transfer the other activities is driven by the strategic understanding of the sector. The following table shows the players in the sector and their competencies on the value chain.

- Some Players across the Value Chain
- SEBs
- Generation, Transmission, and Distribution
- BSES
- Generation and Distribution
- TATA Electricity Companies
- Generation and Distribution
- NTPC
- Thermal Generation

- NHPC
- Hydel Generation
- Gridco
- Transmission
- Power Grid Corporation
- Transmission
- Power Trading Corporation
- Power Trading
- Dabhol Power Company
- Generation
- Wesco, Nesco, Southco Cesco
- Distribution
- AP Transco
- Transmission and Distribution

The Road Ahead

The business scenario of the power sector is at the threshold of huge changes. Un-bundling, integrations, nationalization (like sale of one of the generating units in Orissa to NTPC), privatisation of generation and distribution activities and many such changes will become common. Currently, the power companies deal only in power; however, in the near future they may provide a package of services that include internet service and telecommunication etc.

In India, Power Grid Corporation has already made forays into the telecommunications. In the years to come there is a possibility of some companies further narrowing its operations (like Gridco planning to divide its business into Wheeling and Trading activities) and some other companies further diversify to into newer areas (BSES and AES planning to get into Transmission). Even the company like NTPC whose core competency is in generation is planning to get into the business of distribution. In such situations SCM provides a useful framework to understand the business better and take decisions accordingly.

All manufacturing companies sell their products to make profit. The profit on each product sold can be defined as the difference between the selling price of the product and the total cost of making the product. Cost therefore plays a very important role in the product design process. To be successful, a product must not only satisfy a set of functions defined in the product design specification, but it must also be possible to build the product within the cost criteria set out at the start of the project. Before the development of any product begins, it is essential to perform some form of economic analysis on the product to determine if it is worth making. This may involve some form of market analysis to determine what the customer is willing to pay for a product.

The costs involved in any product can be spilt into development costs and the product cost. Interestingly, some companies do not actually know what their costs are which leaves them open to the possibility that their actual costs may be more than the selling price of their product! An example of this was the Mini when it was first produced in the early 60's. Market research suggested that the car should be sold for less than £500 so the company priced the car at £499. Later when they analysed the cost of producing the car they found that the car cost around £530 to build, resulting in large losses for the manufacturer.

Development Costs

Development costs can be seen as the overheads required to produce all your products and keep your business running. These include costs of market analysis, research and development costs, advertising costs, machine tool costs, storage costs, plant maintenance costs etc. I.e. all the cost that cannot be apportioned to one particular product but are the costs needed for the company to continue to be successful. Decisions regarding development costs are likely to be made by senior management within a company.

Component Costs

The decision as to whether or not to buy a component or service from an outside supplier is a complex one that most designers will be forced to make at some stage. It requires an understanding of the costs associated with making the components in-house and buying the components from a supplier. There may also be company considerations to consider when making the decision. For instance a company may be reluctant to buy components from a competitor even though the cost of manufacture in house may be more than the cost of buying from that competitor.

Some factors which should be considered are:

- How big is the production run? If it is a short run, buying parts from suppliers may prove to be cheaper.
- Can the supplier provide the required number of parts needed?
- If we make it in-house will we have to buy new machines or employ more people?
- The spare parts policy.

Material Costs

The cost of using materials should be has to be considered

Manufacturing Process Costs

The costs of manufacturing processes are dictated by how many parts are to be made using the process. The longer the production run, the more mass production techniques such as automation should be considered.

Casting Costs

Generally the most economic casting process will be dictated by the size of the production run. For small runs, the cost of a pattern for the casting and any set up costs will form a large part of the total casting cost. For larger production runs, the cost of the pattern and set up costs for each individual casting will be very small and material costs will therefore be more important. For small production runs, sand casting is usually the most economical process, while for mass production, die casting and centrifugal casting become more viable. Generally, a casting's costs decreases considerably as the size of the production run increases.

Machining Costs

The cost of machining will depend on the type of material being machined, the amount of material being removed, the size of the component and the size of the production run. For mass production, automated techniques are generally employed to reduce labour costs, however this results in large set up costs.

Fabrication Costs

The costs for fabrication techniques do not decrease significantly with increased production sizes unless the process can be automated. However this implies an increase set up costs.

Welding Costs

Generally for larger production runs, automated techniques are used which result in reduced labour costs but a large initial set up cost due to the having to buy a new machine. Different welding processes imply different costs. MIG and TIG welding are generally more expensive than manual metal arc or oxy - acetylene type welding because of the increased cost of the consumables used and, in the case of TIG, the increased labour costs because of the slower rate of welding.

Bolting Costs

In general, an increase in the number of bolts will result in a more expensive product because of the problems with handling and inserting bolts. Hence, within reason, a smaller number of stronger bolts should be used in preference to a larger number of smaller and therefore weaker bolts. Individual bolt prices will be dictated by the type of material, thread types, nut types etc.

Gluing Costs

The cost of gluing depends on the cost of the glue used and the labour costs. The price of adhesives can vary hugely depending on the type of adhesive. Unless the process is automated, gluing is fairly labour intensive and time consuming because of the care that must be taken in the preparation of the joint and the time necessary for the adhesive to cure or harden. Generally, gluing costs are similar with to other common joining processes such as bolting and welding.

Storage Costs

Traditionally, manufacturers would order stock (e.g. materials and components from outside suppliers) in bulk well in advance of the time when the items would actually be needed.

However, this strategy has a number of limitations in that a large amount of space needs to be set aside for storing stock and also if a particular product line suddenly changes, the organisation could be left with a large amount of unwanted obsolete stock. Hence the concept of 'Just in time' ordering (JIT) has become very popular as a stock control strategy.

The 'Just in time' philosophy involves only ordering items from outside suppliers when the production line imminently needs that item. This limits the problems inherent in the traditional stock ordering process but does introduce problems of it's own. The principal one being that very close ties need to be maintained between an organisation and it's outside suppliers in order to ensure that stock arrives in time.

'Just in time' requires good stock control. Most large organisations now have computerised stock control systems which maintain certain minimum levels of commonly used items, tracking how components are being used and how well the end product is being sold. When the stock level falls below this minimum level, the system will automatically generate a stock order to an outside supplier.

BIBLIOGRAPHY

Belanoff, Pat : *Portfolios: Process and Product,* Poutsmouth, Heinemann, 1991.

Brown, Genevieve: *The Principal Cost Management*, Thousand Oaks, Corwin Press, 1997.

Burke, Kay: *Designing Professional Portfolios for Change*, Palatine, SkyLight Training & Publishing, 1997.

Cater, Erlet, and Gwen Lowman: *Ecotourism: A Sustainable Option?,* New York, John Wiley & Sons, 1994.

Clough, Richard: *Construction Project Management*, New York, John Wiley & Son, 2000.

Debra, Bayles: *The Portfolio Planner - Making Professional Portfolios Work for You,* N.J., Merrill, 1999.

Dickson, Marcia: *Cost Management: Process and Product,* Poutsmouth, Heinemann, 1991.

Frame, J. Davidson: *Managing Projects in Organizations: How to Make the Best Use of Time, Techniques, and People*, San Francisco, Jossey-Bass, 1995.

Goldman, George, and Anthony Nakazawa: *Impact of Visitor Expenditures on Local Revenues*, Corvallis, Oregon, 1994.

Helleiner, Gerald K.: *The Less Developed Countries in the International Economy*, Cambridge, Cambridge University Press, 1975.

Hoffman, Edward: *Project Management Success Stories: Lessons of Project Leaders*, New York, John Wiley & Son, 2000.

Ireland, Lewis: *Quality Management for Projects and Programs*, Upper Darby, PMI, 1991.

Johannis, Theodore B., and C. Neil Bull: *Sociology of Leisure*, California, Sage, 1971.

Kando, Thomas M.: *Leisure and Popular Culture in Transition*, St. Louis, Mosby, 1980.

Kuehn, Diane: *Considerations for Agritourism Development*, New York, Sea Grant, 1998.

Laufer, Alexander : *Project Management Success Stories: Lessons of Project Leaders*, New York, John Wiley & Son, 2000.

Lock, Dennis: *Project Management*, New York, Wiley, 1996.

Pinto, Jeffrey K. and Kharbanda, O.P.: *Successful Project Managers: Leading Your Team to Success*, New York, Van Nostrand Reinhold, 1995.

Rosenburg, Marc J.: *E-Learning: Strategies for Delivering Knowledge in the Digital Age*, New York, McGraw-Hill, 2001.

Rothman, Hal: *Reopening the American West*, Tucson, University of Arizona Press, 1998.

Seldin, Peter: *The Teaching Portfolio*, Bolton, Anker Publishing, 1997.

Shaklee, B. D.: *Designing and Using Portfolios*, Boston, Allyn and Bacon, 1997.

Stefanakis, Evangeline: *Multiple Intelligences and Portfolios: A Window into the Learner's Mind*, Pourtsmouth, Heinemann, 2002.

Wolf, Kenneth: *Leading the Professional Portfolio Process for Change*, Arlington Heights, Skylight Professional Development , 1999.

INDEX

O

P

R

S

T

W